THE
END
OF THE
DAYS

THE
END
OF THE
DAYS

ARTHUR E. BLOOMFIELD

BETHANY HOUSE PUBLISHERS
MINNEAPOLIS, MINNESOTA 55438

The End of the Days
Copyright © 1961
Arthur E. Bloomfield

ISBN 0–7642–2193–0

Cover design by Sheryl Thornberg

Published by Bethany House Publishers
A Ministry of Bethany Fellowship International
11400 Hampshire Avenue South
Minneapolis, Minnesota 55438
www.bethanyhouse.com

Printed in the United States of America by
Bethany Press International, Minneapolis, Minnesota 55438

CONTENTS

CONTENTS

CONTENTS

LIST OF CHARTS AND MAPS

Page

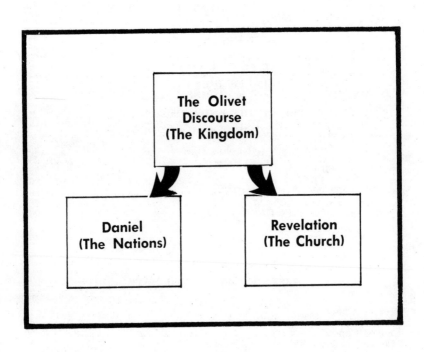

But go thou thy way till the end be: for thou shalt rest, and stand in thy lot **at the end of the days.** —Dan. 12:13.

PREFACE

The three prophecies—Daniel, The Olivet Discourse, and Revelation—form a prophetic trilogy. In the Olivet Discourse, Jesus reached back to Daniel and forward to Revelation, and without unnecessary repetition, combined the three into a consonant whole; it is the bridge that unites Daniel and Revelation. Although we have printed our studies of these prophecies in three volumes, we have thought of them as one revelation.

In this book I have dealt only with the prophetic portions of Daniel; the rest is self-explanatory. I am sorry that at times I have had to depart from the usual interpretations, which have never helped our understanding. The nearer we come to the actual events the greater will be our understanding and the more amazing these prophecies will seem. Daniel is written especially for "the end of the days." "The wise *shall* understand" (Dan. 12:10). When that time comes, these prophecies will have an evangelistic appeal, and "they that be wise shall shine as the brightness of the firmament; and they that turn many to righteousness as the stars for ever and ever" (Dan. 12:3).

Arthur E. Bloomfield

Eustis, Florida
July 1961

INTRODUCTION

INTRODUCTION

THE PROPHETIC METHOD

Prophecy has been defined as history written in advance. This is somewhat of an oversimplification, for prophecy is more than this. If God wants a certain message to be given to a certain people at a certain time in the future, He does not have to wait until that time comes, and then hurry to get someone to write the message and circulate it. Thousands of years before, God could (and did) cause the message to be written, printed, and put in wide circulation when the time for its use should come.

The Bible has special messages for people of all times. The great religious leaders have been men who have found in the Bible the particular message for their day and who then have proclaimed this to the world. For instance, Peter found Old Testament prophecies of the Resurrection and of the outpouring of the Spirit, so his sermon at Pentecost was made up almost entirely of those prophecies. Likewise, Martin Luther proclaimed a truth not new to the Bible but new to the people of Luther's day—justification by faith. This truth, however, was not itself prophecy, but originally came from the prophecy of Habakkuk: "The just shall live by his faith" (2:4).

Psalm 91 is actually prophecy. In days to come when the 144,000 Israelites on Mount Zion (surrounded by the carnage of the plagues of fire, by the devastation caused by evil spirits, and by the armed threat of the forces of Antichrist) will be gathered together having the seal of God's protection, then they will be able to open the Bible and read Psalm 91. This Psalm was written *for* them and *about* them—written thousands of years before—and cherished through the ages as a spiritual truth of great comfort. But only then can it be literally applied. Thus Psalm 91 will yet be literally fulfilled prophecy. It is more than history written in advance. It is the words and experiences of a people. It is the very thoughts of their hearts perfectly expressed. Read the Psalm with this in mind.

> He that dwelleth in the secret place of the most High shall abide under the shadow of the Almighty. I will say of the Lord, He is my refuge and my fortress: my God; in him will I trust.
> Surely he shall deliver thee from the snare of the fowler, and from the noisome pestilence. He shall cover thee with his feathers, and under his wings shalt thou trust: his truth shall be thy shield and buckler.
> Thou shalt not be afraid for the terror by night; nor for the arrow that flieth by day; nor for the pestilence that walketh in darkness; nor for the destruction that wasteth at noonday. A thousand shall fall at thy side, and ten thousand at thy right hand; but it shall not come nigh thee.
> Only with thine eyes shalt thou behold and see the reward of the wicked. Because thou hast made the Lord, which is my refuge, even the most High, thy habitation; there shall no evil befall thee, neither shall any plague come nigh thy dwelling. —Ps. 91:1–10.

God has a terrific message in the Bible for the end of the age, which will be the climax of all the ages. This special message is found in the prophetic Scriptures; in fact, the end of the age is almost the whole content of the prophetic Scriptures. It will stir the world, because even as it will be preached, it will be in process of fulfillment.

No miracle is more sensational than prophecy when it is being fulfilled. A large portion of the Bible is pointed at these "end days." Its message is clear, concise, and as detailed as though it had been written at the very time.

At present there is some confusion in prophetic study. This is caused by two things: First, there is so much material; the details are so many that there will need to be organization and harmony. Second, there has been too much prophetic "teaching" not found in the Bible. Too many statements have been made without Scriptural support. Therefore, it is going to be necessary for us to proceed on the following basis:

No matter how many people believe a statement—
No matter how many great Bible teachers say it—
No matter how many books it is in—
If it is not in the Bible, it could be wrong.

This may sound axiomatic, yet the fact is that it would put a question mark after about nine-tenths of what we have been taught along some lines. This is actually a serious situation. For that reason, our first purpose must be to bring together the Scriptures themselves and apply them to the proper times.

The Bible is not primarily history but a revelation from God to every age, and written especially for that age; prophecy, therefore, is not primarily history but a revelation from God to a certain age. All revelation from God is useful in all ages, but there is one time when each revelation or prophecy may be finally and literally applied. Only when it is applied to the right time may a prophecy be completely comprehended.

THE LANGUAGE OF PROPHECY

The language of prophecy has certain characteristics and forms that make reading it almost like learning to read a new language. This learning the characteristics of prophecy is quite necessary, because requirements for prophecy are different. For instance, the prophets must use the vocabulary of their own day to express thoughts that had never entered the mind of man. Thus they had to find means

of calling by name people and countries which would not
come into being for thousands of years. Some conception
may be had of the difficulties involved in such a procedure
by simply imagining someone trying to tell George Washington about radio or television without using any words
that he did not know.

The prophets continually speak of conditions and things
unknown in their own day. Isaiah describes airplanes as
horses flying with wheels like a whirlwind, and roaring
like lions (Isa. 5:28, 29).* The prophet Nahum tells what
he saw in "the day of his preparation"—preparation for the
coming of Christ: "The chariots shall rage in the streets,
they shall justle one against another in the broad ways: they
shall seem like torches, they shall run like the lightnings"
(Nah. 2:4).

All these are some of the simpler problems. Somewhat
more difficult to express in advance would be the movements
of empires into new parts of the world, the rise and fall of
kingdoms, the revival of ancient lands, the discovery of new
kinds of wealth, the coming of new religions, prosperity of a
new kind, great scientific developments, new kinds of warfare (a cold war, for instance), and the spread of communism.

Yet all these descriptions would be easy compared to
putting into words such spiritual things as the Resurrection,
the experiences of the saints in heaven, the return of Christ
and His millennial reign, as well as all prophecies concerning Satan, Antichrist, and evil spirits. No language on earth
has words to express what the prophets saw.

Usually the prophets could not invent new words, for
such would have no meaning. Yet on occasion, the writers
of the Bible did this very thing, but these words are either

*Whose arrows are sharp, and all their bows bent, their horses' hoofs shall
be counted like flint, and their wheels like a whirlwind: Their roaring shall be
like a lion, they shall roar like young lions: yea, they shall roar, and lay hold of
the prey, and shall carry it away safe, and none shall deliver it. —Isa. 5:28, 29.

left untranslated, or are translated by some word that does not convey the exact meaning. For instance, after Amalek's defeat, Moses called the altar of thanksgiving "Jehovah-nissi" (Ex. 17:15). *Nissi,* in this passage, is not translated because there is no equivalent word for it; in other places it is translated "banner," "standard," "pole," and "ensign"; but even these words do not exactly express the meaning. Likewise, in Genesis 6:4 we read, "There were *giants* in the earth in those days." The Hebrew for giants is "nephilim," which does not mean giants, but is the best word the translators could find. "Fallen ones" would probably be a better translation, or the Hebrew word "nephilim" should be left untranslated. "There were *nephilim* in the earth in those days."

Usually the prophets expressed their thoughts in words of known meaning. These would some day make sense, but in the prophet's day had an application unknown. One of the marvels of the Bible is the ingenious way in which the prophets used words whose meaning would become known only in the day of fulfillment.

We may divide the prophets' methods of expression into two groups: *figurative* and *literal.* The figurative is the easier to understand; the literal offers more difficulties; therefore, we will first consider the figurative language.

Figurative Language

Figurative language may, in turn, be divided into two groups: types and symbols.

TYPES

A type is usually some person or thing that actually lived or existed and that had a single counterpart or anti-type in the future. In this it differs from a symbol. As a group, types differ from symbols in several respects, but the principal difference between a type and a symbol lies in the manner of interpretation. A type *must* be like the antitype in *some* respects, *but in these respects only* is it a type. It is never like the antitype in *all* respects. For instance, Adam is a type of Christ—that is, there are some points of similarity between Adam and Christ; and in these points only, Adam is a type. Adam was not a type of Christ when he was hiding from God. Similarly, Eve, the wife of Adam, may be considered a type of the Church, the bride of Christ. In *some* respects Jonah's experiences were similar to Christ's, in *others* they were not; nevertheless, Jonah is a type of Christ.

In the Old Testament there are many such types, with their antitypes in the New Testament. (For instance, Adam is a type of Christ; Jonah is a type of Christ.) In the New Testament there are a few types. In Revelation, the seven churches are types because in some respects they are like the churches which they prefigure. (To be types, they do not have to be *exactly* like the future churches, but in *some* respects must be like the antitypes.) Whether the seven churches are types of the Church in various ages has been disputed because the correspondence is not perfect. But no type ever corresponded perfectly with the antitype. Therefore, the seven churches *are* perfect types, even though the similarity is limited.

Inasmuch as the type is like the counterpart only in certain respects, it is impossible to understand a type until the antitype has arrived and comparison can be made. A study of types is very useful, but care should be taken not to go beyond that which is intended.

SYMBOLS

A symbol is the arbitrary use of *one* object to indicate *another*. It is a symbol because it is declared to be so. Any one thing can be a symbol of anything else. For example, the kingdom of heaven is said to be like unto seed, or like unto treasure hid in a field, etc. Symbols are so common that they should give us little trouble. The nations have always used symbols to depict themselves—an eagle, a lion, a bear, a crescent, a serpent. Today the political parties use symbols even on the election ballots. All cartoons are made up of symbols. However, symbols need not in any way be actually like the thing which they represent. They have a given meaning with no reference to similarities. Interpretation, therefore, is not by means of comparison. Moreover, a seed, a stone, buried treasure, a pearl, a fish, and a man child may all be symbols of the same thing.

Symbols are not peculiar to the Bible, and are older than the Bible; in fact, they are one of the first things mentioned in the Bible. In Genesis 1:14, God said, "Let there be lights . . . ; *and let them be for signs.*"

The oldest known symbols are the signs of the zodiac. ("The zodiac is an imaginary belt of the heavens within which are the apparent paths of the sun, moon, and principal planets. It contains twelve constellations and hence twelve signs or symbols." —*Dictionary.*) These signs are the same in all lands of the earth, indicating that they came from that early time when all the world was of one language. Although now their real symbolic meaning is lost, they once constituted a revelation from God. The use (for evil purpose) of some such great knowledge caused God at the tower of Babel to send the confusion of tongues. Nothing short of this evil could have been responsible for such extreme language as we have in Genesis 11:6: "The Lord said, Behold, the people is one, and they have all one language; and this they begin to do; and now nothing will be restrained from them, which they have imagined to do."

Unless a symbol is explained in some way, it cannot be understood. A cartoonist labels some but not necessarily all of his symbols; some may be understood from those already explained. So likewise, in Matthew Chapter 13, Jesus explained some but not all of His symbols, for all will be readily understood if we apply the knowledge obtained from those that were explained. In the Bible, symbols are usually explained the first time they are used, but not in succeeding occurrences. For instance, the meaning of the lion, the bear, the leopard, and the beast is given to us in the book of Daniel; but later on in the Bible where these same symbols are repeated in Revelation, the meaning is *not* given.

Symbols, unlike types, may be understood *before* they are fulfilled; in fact, that is the function of a symbol—to express something that is still future (except in the case of memorials). Symbolism is the easiest way of expressing a future occurrence, for through the years symbols do not change, and suffer less in translation. Moreover, for symbols, names of people and places do not have to be known in advance. To name the people and places might defeat the prophecy; it has to be so expressed that it will not influence the prophesied event adversely.

An illustration of how prophecy *could* influence the event if actual names are used is seen in the prediction of Isaiah that Cyrus would set the Jews free to return and rebuild Jerusalem (Isaiah 44:28).* Cyrus was so impressed by the prophecy that he lost no time in carrying out its provisions. In other cases, such a prophecy is so worded that those whom it involves are not conscious of fulfilling it and so are not able to prevent its fulfillment. It is in this respect that symbols are most useful.

Symbols are easier to understand than any "plain words" that could be used. An illustration of this is found in the four visions of Daniel. Daniel Chapters 2, 7, and 8, where symbols are used, are much easier to understand than Chapter 11, which covers the same ground without symbols, and is therefore harder to understand. Thus, when we are looking far into the future, names of people and places would

---

*That saith of Cyrus, He is my shepherd, and shall perform all my pleasure: even saying to Jerusalem, Thou shalt be built; and to the temple, Thy foundation shall be laid. — Isa. 44:28.

mean nothing; working conditions would be so much different as to be unexpressible. But symbols are the easiest way out of this difficulty.

It is possible for the same thing to be both a type and a symbol. A lamb is an example. A lamb is made a symbol of Christ. A lamb's effectiveness for the remission of sin lay solely in the fact that it was symbolical of Christ. Yet the symbol took on the features of a type. A lamb has many points of similarity to Christ, such as innocence, humility, obedience. Its fulfillment follows that of a symbol. Thus one thing (e.g., lamb) could be entirely different from that of which it is a figure (Christ), and so would be a symbol; yet at the same time it might have similarities that would make it a type. Sometimes, too, a symbol becomes so common that it actually becomes a name. This is also illustrated in the case of the lamb, for in Revelation the most used name of Christ is the Lamb.

Action in symbols

In symbolical language where there is action added to the symbol, the action is always literal. The method of interpretation will be to determine the meaning of the symbols and then apply the action literally. For instance, Jesus said, "The kingdom of heaven is likened unto leaven which a woman took and hid in three measures of meal." Whatever the woman stands for *took* whatever the leaven stands for and *hid* it in whatever the meal stands for. Or, in Revelation Chapter 12, whatever the woman stands for *gave birth* to whatever the man child stands for, and whatever the man child stands for was *caught up* into heaven. In every case the action is literal. The same is true of the lamb. The applied action portrays the sacrifice of Christ.

Heavenly things are not symbolized. Sometimes things in heaven seem like symbols, and there is a tendency to treat them as such; but there is a better way of interpreting those things. For instance, in Revelation Chapter 12 mentioned above, the woman is a symbol, the man child is a symbol; but God and His throne are *not* symbols. As soon as the action leaves the earth and passes into heaven, the language becomes literal.

Literal Language

Here again we have two groups: heavenly and earthly—that is, language that concerns heavenly things and experiences, and language that concerns earthly things and experiences. This is a most important distinction. It is at this point that so many teachers have gone astray in their interpretations.

HEAVENLY LANGUAGE

For understanding words, we depend upon our experiences. You may say to a child, "The stove is hot," but until the child has felt something hot or has been burned, he will not know what "hot" means. A new word, expressing something completely beyond our experience, would have no meaning to us unless something in its root or in its sound connected it with something in our experience.

Many things in heaven are entirely beyond our experience. They are things that "eye hath not seen, nor ear heard, neither hath entered into the heart of man." Their understanding is only through the Spirit, for there are no human words to express these things. For instance, there are no words to translate what the prophet Ezekiel saw when he, like John, was caught up into heaven. And the Apostle Paul, who also had such an experience, said that it was simply impossible to relate what he saw. On the other hand, the Apostle John was told, "Write what thou seest."

There is only one way that heavenly things could be expressed—that is, to use the nearest corresponding earthly word. Sometimes this is not very near. Thus, when Ezekiel described the cherubim, he was not using symbols, for the cherubim are not symbols of something on earth, but are a heavenly group, or organization, or "machine." But for this heavenly group there is no earthly word. The wings, the faces, the wheels in Ezekiel are whatever in heaven would correspond to those things on earth (and probably the correspondence is not very close). Nevertheless, when once the method is recognized, a great deal may be learned from these heavenly scenes. Certainly nothing whatever can be learned by treating these wonderful pictures of scenes in heaven as though they were symbols of something on earth. The transparent gold of the holy city is not a symbol of something down here. John saw whatever in that heavenly city corresponds in value and beauty to gold.

The scene of a large part of Revelation is laid in heaven, and heavenly things are not symbolized. To treat as symbols the throne of God, the book with seven seals, the elders, the living ones, the horsemen, and the angels, is to throw the whole book into confusion. These are *heavenly* things and *heavenly* beings. Some of them may have come from the earth, for they say they are redeemed from every nation, but they are in heaven and are immortal. They do things in heaven, and they do things to the earth from heaven. They are not symbols of earthly things, but are very real, literal, heavenly beings. And the things they do are real and literal.

We have to recognize heavenly things as heavenly things. It is at this point that many interpreters become confused, for they fail to recognize heavenly things as such and try to make heavenly things symbols of earthly things. The Bible deals with heaven as well as with earth, and we must learn to translate heavenly language.

EARTHLY LANGUAGE

It is strange that in the use of literal language we should have fallen into so many errors, which have been responsible for some unnecessary disputes. Two such errors are these:

(1) using words not found in the Bible; (2) using Bible words but not in the Bible sense.

Words Not Found in the Bible

People will not quarrel with the Bible, so we invent ways of getting truth out of the Bible where it can be debated. Many of the doctrines that divide the churches are expressed in terms not found in the Bible.

All Christian doctrines and beliefs are expressed in the Bible, and the Bible is written in words; therefore we *should* be able to express all our beliefs in Bible words. Any belief that can *not* be expressed in Bible words is open to question.

Some extra-Biblical words, such as rapture (which certainly expresses a Bible truth) are very useful, but when controversy arises over the Rapture or some features of it, it becomes necessary to return the doctrine to the Bible and insist upon the use of Bible words only. That would settle most disputes.

Words Not Used in the Bible Sense

When we use Bible words, it is necessary that we use them with the Bible meaning. Even though we use Bible words, if we put new meanings on them not found in the Bible, we have lost the Bible teaching.

In present-day prophetic teaching, the meaning of some key words has been changed, so that what we are talking about is not what the Bible is talking about. Naturally, that throws us into confusion. In a writing of this kind, there are certain Bible words and expressions that cannot be used at will, because they are so treated in modern-day literature that their meanings no longer correspond with their use in the Bible. The logical way would be to return these words and phrases to the Bible and use them in the Bible sense; the human way is to start an argument.

(1) *Use of the word tribulation.* An example of a word not used in the Bible sense is the word *tribulation.* This word,

in the Bible, is *not* the name of a period of time. Certain phrases, on the other hand, like "the twentieth century" and "the day of the Lord," are names of periods of time, so that whenever you say twentieth century, you mean the exact time, and whenever the Bible says "day of the Lord," it always refers to the same general time. The word *tribulation* is not such a word, but like the word *persecution,* refers to an experience that people are passing through. Tribulation may come any time. Jesus said, "In the world ye shall have tribulation"; and, "Ye shall have tribulation ten days." Every time the Bible uses the word *tribulation,* it does not refer to the same time but to *a similar experience.* Tribulation is not like such expressions as "Daniel's 70th Week," which always refers to the same time wherever we see it used.

Jesus spoke of the "tribulation of those days" (Matt. 24:29).* You would not speak of the twentieth century of those days, or the day of the Lord of those days. The very fact that Jesus spoke of the tribulation *of those days* indicated there are other tribulations. In Matthew 24:29 Jesus was referring to the troubles or sorrows of those days, using the word not as the name of a certain period of time but merely as referring to the experiences of the people he is talking about.

Tribulation may come at any time, and there may be more than one time of great tribulation. Different peoples have tribulation—the Jews have tribulation; the saints have tribulation; those saved after the Resurrection have tribulation. These would not all have to come at the same time, because *tribulation does not refer to a specific time.*

Tribulation usually refers to people being persecuted because of their religion or race. In Revelation, the word *tribulation* is *not* used of the nations that are caught in the

---

*Immediately after the tribulation of those days shall the sun be darkened, and the moon shall not give her light, and the stars shall fall from heaven, and the powers of the heavens shall be shaken. —Matt. 24:29.

judgments of God; it is *not* used of the seven last plagues, the trumpets and vials. Tribulation is used only in reference to the persecution of the saints who will be saved after the Resurrection, and in this respect they may be called "tribulation saints." In Revelation, the word *tribulation* is used of these particular persecuted people and of these people only. It is *never* used to name the time that comes between the Resurrection and the return of Christ, but only to the troubles that the saints go through during a portion of that time.

When Jesus used the word *tribulation* in the Olivet Discourse, He was not necessarily referring to the same time, because He was talking about a different people. Two periods of tribulation could be the same *length* of time and still not be the same time.

We talk about pre-, mid-, and post-tribulation Rapture, which gives us a beautiful subject for controversy with which to confuse the minds of listeners. In order to have such a subject for controversy, we have to do two things: first, use a word that is not in the Bible (i.e., rapture); second, use a Bible word *in a sense* that is not found in the Bible. We can debate that forever and not get anywhere. The simple solution, but not the human one, would be to use only Bible words and to use Bible words only in their Bible meanings.

(2) *Use of the word rapture.* The word *rapture* is so useful that I hesitate to discard it. I think it may safely be used (except when controversy arises). There is, however, one other danger in its use. Whenever a new word displaces a Bible word (or words), we may lose something that is latent in the displaced words, something that is necessary for the full understanding of the subject. The use of the word *rapture* has not, in itself, led to any misunderstanding, but the failure to recognize and use certain Bible words is causing some trouble. Another controversy is sure to a-

rise which could have been avoided by the simple practice of using Bible expressions in their Bible meanings.

Of course the word *rapture* expresses a Bible truth, but the writers of the Bible had to express that same truth without the use of that word. They had to find other words. They did not confine themselves to a single word as we are doing, but used a number of words and expressions which tell more than is contained in the word *rapture*. We should be careful that we do not replace those words and thereby miss some of the truth, especially as this leads to the misunderstanding of other parts of Scripture. To misunderstand one truth always hides other truths.

Many of the Bible words for rapture are verbs which are awkward to use as nouns. The resurrection is a twofold operation, involving the dead as well as the living. The dead are raised; the living are caught up. Here again we use verbs. For the verb *raised,* there is the noun *resurrection;* but there seems to be no noun for *caught up.* Paul came close to it when he spoke of "our gathering together unto him." In this expression there is a thought not found in the word *rapture.* In the added word *together* is expressed a "gathering together," a "reunion of the saints"—not only a union with Christ but a reunion with each other. In place of rapture, the phrase "our gathering together unto him" could be used, but it is a little too long for most people in the twentieth century.

(3) *Use of the word resurrection.* The word *resurrection* is short enough, but it is deficient in that it does *not* include the living who are not raised up but caught up. Moreover, in Revelation, the term *the first resurrection* includes the tribulation saints, who will be raised (if they are killed) and included in the first resurrection. So in one way the word *resurrection* included not all that we mean, and in another way, more than we mean.

Nevertheless, in this book I am using resurrection as synonymous with rapture.

(4) *Use of the word redemption.* For rapture, Jesus used the word *redemption*—"your redemption." He said, "When these things begin to come to pass, then look up, and lift up your heads; for *your redemption* draweth nigh" (Luke 21:28). Here redemption does not mean salvation. We who are saved still look for the redemption of the body. "And not only they, but ourselves also, which have the firstfruits of the Spirit, even we ourselves groan within ourselves, waiting for the adoption, to wit, *the redemption of our body*" (Romans 8:23). "And grieve not the holy Spirit of God, whereby ye are sealed unto *the day of redemption*" (Eph. 4:30).

"Our redemption" would be a good substitute for rapture. The rapture is our redemption. But Jesus said, "When these things *begin* to come to pass, then look up and lift up your heads, for your redemption draweth nigh." Some things will happen first. Some things we will see. There are signs of our redemption. The first things Jesus mentioned were the rise of many false Christs and the hearing of wars and commotions. Later, Jesus mentioned some other things: "As it was in the days of Noah, so shall also the coming of the Son of man be." This is followed by a detailed account of the "catching up" (Matt. 24:37–42).*

Some of the most amazing things about the day of redemption are completely lost to us because of a disregard of, or a refusal to believe certain Bible statements—clean-cut, precise statements which are still completely outside our doctrine of the Rapture. Because we have substituted the word rapture for the Bible words, we have missed their meaning.

---

*But as the days of Noe were, so shall also the coming of the Son of man be. For as in the days that were before the flood they were eating and drinking, marrying and giving in marriage, until the day that Noe entered into the ark, and knew not until the flood came, and took them all away; so shall also the coming of the Son of man be.

Then shall two be in the field; the one shall be taken, and the other left. Two women shall be grinding at the mill; the one shall be taken, and the other left. Watch therefore: for ye know not what hour your Lord doth come. —Matt. 24:37–42.

An example of how the replacing of a Bible word with one of our own can lead us into an unscriptural position is seen in the modern tendency to think and teach that all prophecy is for the Jews, and that there is nothing for the Church to look for except the Resurrection. The fact is, a large segment of prophecy, including the return of the Jews, could be fulfilled *before* the saints are caught up. Will anyone say that the recovery of Palestine and the return of a million and a half Jews is not the beginning of the fulfillment of prophecies concerning the return of the Jews? Nevertheless, the saints are not yet "caught up," but are still here. If a prophecy could be partially fulfilled, could it not be totally fulfilled? "Shall I bring to birth and not cause to bring forth? saith the Lord." This error of replacing the Bible word with one of our own could be avoided by using a Bible word in place of rapture, or rather by not using rapture in place of a Bible word.

Study 1

THE TIME ELEMENT

THE TIME ELEMENT

In order to understand any prophecy, one must have the answers to four standard questions: Who? What? Where? When? The text usually tells *who* and *what,* and it is not so difficult to determine *where* the action is to take place. The big question is always *when.*

If there is confusion in understanding prophecy, it is usually caused by putting the prophecy in the wrong place. A misplaced prophecy is a misunderstood prophecy every time. Sometimes commentaries try to explain a prophecy by applying it to some past event or series of events, and then have to admit that it only partially fits. They put all the blame on the prophet, saying that he is using hyperbole— which according to the dictionary means "obvious exaggeration for effect."

But the prophets did not have to use exaggeration for effect or for any other reason. Most prophecy is understatement; the fulfillment far exceeds the terms of the prophecy. Prophecy deals, for the most part, with situations that are impossible to exaggerate. For example, there are no words to express the terror of "the day of the Lord" or "the glory that shall be revealed in us."

The reason a prophecy seems to be an exaggeration is that it is being applied to the wrong time. We do not have to know calendar dates, "the times or the seasons which the Father hath put in his own power," but we do need to have the time of one prophecy in proper relationship to an-

other. To arrive at a proper sequence of events would probably clear up more "hard places" in prophecy than any other
single accomplishment, and bring order out of confusion.

A chronological harmony of prophetic events should
make it possible eventually to put all prophecy in chronological order. This would end all present-day confusion and make
possible a united, concerted, and detailed study of prophecy.

But this is not a simple matter. The subject has been
complicated yet further by the fact that there have been
firmly implanted in our minds many ideas which cannot be
supported by Scripture and therefore could be wrong.

History sometimes repeats itself. Many places have
passed through a number of similar experiences. Because
some predictions about the future of such places as Jerusalem and Tyre are much like their past, the prophecy may
seem to apply to both. We have therefore developed a theory
of double fulfillment. But there is a better method of interpretation. *A prophecy actually applies to one time only*, for
although two events may be similar, they are not identical.
In order to apply a prophecy to the wrong place, there always has to be some distortion either of prophecy or of history (usually a little of both). The prophets themselves were
never confused.

The time of a prophecy can be determined by rule. One
simple rule is this: *If a prophecy has never yet been completely fulfilled, then it is to be fulfilled in the future.*

The Old Testament prophetical books may be grouped
into two general classes: (1) those that deal with *both* their
own times *and* the future; (2) those that deal *only* with the
future. There is no guesswork here. The prophets themselves
indicate in which group their writings fall. If a book is to
treat of its own times, it is necessary to know what those
times are; therefore the book will begin by stating the date
and place. For instance: "The vision of Isaiah the son of
Amoz, which he saw concerning Judah and Jerusalem in the

days of Uzziah, Jotham, Ahaz, and Hezekiah, kings of Judah"
(Isa. 1:1).

If, however, a prophecy is concerning the future only,
there is no need for a statement as to its time and place.
When these are omitted, the book is concerned only with
the time of the end. For instance: "The vision of Obadiah.
Thus saith the Lord God concerning Edom; We have heard a
rumour from the Lord, and an ambassador is sent among
the heathen, Arise ye, and let us rise up against her in battle"
(Obad. 1:1).

This groups the prophets as follows:

Both current and future		All future
Isaiah	Amos	Joel
Jeremiah	Micah	Obadiah
Ezekiel	Zephaniah	Nahum
Daniel	Haggai	Habakkuk
Hosea	Zechariah	Malachi

(Zephaniah has only a little concerning his own time. Zech-
ariah mentions the time but not the place; his prophecy is
nearly all future.)

Never distort a prophecy in the least to make it fit some
past event, for to do so always hides a truth. To put a
prophecy in its right time not only helps to clear up that passage, but usually throws light on other passages also. The
fact is that in all prophecies relating to the last days, time
indicators are present. The prophets used a number of devices to time their prophecies. You need only to know these
simple rules to time any prophecy. One way to indicate time
is *by special terms*—for instance, "the day of the Lord,"
"that day," etc. Another way to indicate time is *by association with known events.*

SPECIAL TERMS

"The Day of the Lord"

The formula "the day of the Lord," with certain variations, is used both in the Old and New Testaments as a time indicator. The phrase "the day of the Lord" always dates a prophecy as referring to a future time. The time is the end of the age. Either the Age of Grace or of Law could be in view because both end at approximately the same time. Daniel's 70th week is the end time for the old dispensation, and is almost identical with "the day of the Lord." *The day of the Lord" is a specific time* in that it relates to the events leading up to the coming of Christ in glory. Sometimes it has a special reference to a part of that time such as "the time of Jacob's trouble" (which is usually supposed to be a reference to the last half of Daniel's 70th week).

In some instances, the term "the day of the Lord" may include things that may come before the Rapture and extend briefly into the millennium. In any case, the term is sufficiently specific for its purpose—namely, to take the prophecy out of the past and put it into the future. All prophecy has a goal—the consummation of redemption. It all looks forward to a comparatively brief time when the battle of the earth reaches a climax and the end is near—not the end of the physical earth (there is no such thing), but the end of the battle with Satan when the kingdoms of the world will become the kingdoms of our Lord. That is "the day of the Lord."

> The great day of the Lord is near, it is near, and hasteth greatly, even the voice of the day of the Lord: the mighty man shall cry there bitterly. That day is a day of wrath, a day of trouble and distress, a day of wasteness and desolation, a day of darkness and gloominess, a day of clouds and thick darkness, a day of the trumpet and alarm against the fenced cities, and against the high towers. —Zeph. 1:14–16.

The prophets did not confine themselves to the exact limitations of the "day of the Lord." Sometimes they also saw things which led up to that day. For instance, Obadiah tells what will happen when the "day of the Lord" is near. The trouble between the Arabs and the Jews will come to a head before the "day of the Lord": "For the day of the Lord is near upon all the nations" (Obad. 15, R.V.). So the rule is this: *If the prophecy is related to "the day of the Lord," it is future.*

There is no difference between "the day of Christ" (II Thess. 2:2) * and "the day of the Lord." This is merely a different translation of the same expression. The oldest manuscripts read "day of the Lord."

There are some variations to the phrase "day of the Lord"—"the time of the end," "in the last days," "afterward," (Joel 2:28) § etc., which have the same effect.

"That Day"

The term "that day" with variations, has a very special use in the Old Testament prophecies. It always looks forward to the "day of the Lord," never back to what the prophet has been talking about. It always starts a new thought.

"That day" indicates a change of subject or a new phase of the subject. It is necessary to get the prophet's point of view. He is looking into the future two or three thousand years. But God's telescope works somewhat differently from those which men construct. Whether we are looking into a distance of space or of time, to us the nearest things are seen with the greatest clarity and detail. The farther away we look the more area comes into view at one time, and the less detail is visible.

But with God the greatest detail may come with views that reach into the greatest distance; in fact, the closer we

---

*That ye be not soon shaken in mind, or be troubled, neither by spirit, nor by word, nor by letter as from us, as that the day of Christ is at hand. —II Thess. 2:3.

§ And it shall come to pass afterward, that I will pour out my spirit upon all flesh; and your sons and your daughters shall prophesy, your old men shall dream dreams, your young men shall see visions. —Joel 2:28.

come to "the end," the greater is the detail. Sometimes the prophets deal with the most distant subjects with amazing attention to the smallest details.

If a prophet attempted to tell the whole story of the future and put in all details as he went along, he would find himself going down so many side-roads that he would lose all contact with the main-line issue. The prophets never allow themselves to become sidetracked. They leave all sideline subjects for special treatment. After they have told their story, they go back and fill in the details that have been left out. They indicate this by starting with the formula *"in that day,"* or *"at that time."* Though it might seem that the prophet is connecting his thought with what he has just said, this is *not* the case. The prophet means that he has completed what he has been talking about and is now starting a new thought connected with another part of the story. He has gone back to fill in a detail.

A very important illustration of this rule may be seen in Daniel 12: 1:

> *And at that time* shall Michael stand up, the great prince which standeth for the children of thy people: and there shall be a time of trouble, such as never was since there was a nation even to that same time: and *at that time* thy people shall be delivered, every one that shall be found written in the book.

The commentators stumble over this phrase, "at that time." They argue, "How can it be that after Antichrist has been destroyed and the kingdom of Christ has come, there is a time of trouble such as never was since there was a nation?" But Jesus quoted this statement in Matthew 24: 4 and applied it to the same time as Daniel 11, not afterwards. The fact is that in Daniel 12: 1 "at that time" does *not* mean at the end of the events of Daniel 11. The prophet means that he is going to go back to fill in a detail left out in the main sequence.

Jesus did the same thing in the Olivet Discourse. The details of the Rapture He left out of the main sequence; then He added them at the end. This is the only possible way of telling any story where a number of things are happening at the same time. They have to be told one at a time. This may make it seem as if one follows the other in point of time. When prophets deal with a series of events which overlap as to time, they indicate that fact by starting each separate subject with some such expression as "in that day."

TIMES SET BY ASSOCIATION WITH KNOWN EVENTS

Another way of indicating time is to associate the prophecy with some event whose time is known. For instance, though the time of the fulfillment of Ezekiel 38 and 39 is in much dispute, there is no confusion in the prophecy itself. God says, "This is the day *whereof I have spoken*" (Ezek. 39:8). Again, "Art thou he *of whom I have spoken* in old time by my servants the prophets?" (Ezek. 38:17). In these two chapters in Ezekiel are many places where the prophecy connects with known events.

Compare the following three passages:

And I will call for a sword against him throughout all my mountains, saith the Lord God: every man's sword shall be against his brother. —Ezek. 38:21.

And I will overthrow the throne of kingdoms, and I will destroy the strength of the kingdoms of the heathen; and I will overthrow the chariots, and those that ride in them; and the horses and their riders shall come down, every one by the sword of his brother. —Hag. 2:22.

And it shall come to pass in that day, that a great tumult from the Lord shall be among them; and they shall lay hold every one on the hand of his neighbour, and his hand shall rise up against the hand of his neighbour. —Zech. 14:13.

Compare Ezekiel 39:17–20 with Revelation 19:17–19.

And thou son of man, thus saith the Lord God; Speak unto every feathered fowl, and to every beast

of the field, Assemble yourselves, and come; gather
yourselves on every side to my sacrifice that I do sacrifice
for you, even a great sacrifice upon the mountains of
Israel, that ye may eat flesh, and drink blood.

Ye shall eat the flesh of the mighty, and drink the
blood of the princes of the earth, of rams, of lambs, and
of goats, of bullocks, all of them fatlings of Bashan. And
ye shall eat fat till ye be full, and drink blood till ye be
drunken, of my sacrifice which I have sacrificed for you.
—Ezek. 39:17–20.

And I saw an angel standing in the sun; and he
cried with a loud voice, saying to all the fowls that fly
in the midst of heaven, Come and gather yourselves
together unto the supper of the great God; that ye may
eat the flesh of kings, and the flesh of captains, and the
flesh of mighty men, and the flesh of horses, and of
them that sit on them, and the flesh of all men, both free
and bond, both small and great.

And I saw the beast, and the kings of the earth,
and their armies, gathered together to make war against
him that sat on the horse, and against his army.
—Rev. 19:17–19.

We know from many sources that Israel will be saved
as a nation *after the return of Christ.*

In that day shall the Lord defend the inhabitants
of Jerusalem; and he that is feeble among them at that
day shall be as David; and the house of David shall be
as God, as the angel of the Lord before them. And it shall
come to pass in that day, that I will seek to destroy all
the nations that come against Jerusalem.

And I will pour upon the house of David, and upon
the inhabitants of Jerusalem, the spirit of grace and of
supplications: and they shall look upon me whom they
have pierced, and they shall mourn for him, as one
mourneth for his only son, and shall be in bitterness
for him, as one that is in bitterness for his firstborn.
—Zech. 12:8–10.

Ezekiel associates his prophecy with the return of Christ:

And I will set my glory among the heathen, and all
the heathen shall see my judgment that I have executed,

and my hand that I have laid upon them. So the house of Israel shall know that I am the Lord their God from that day forward.

Then shall they know that I am the Lord their God, which caused them to be led into captivity among the heathen: but I have gathered them unto their own land, and have left none of them any more there. Neither will I hide my face any more from them: for I have poured out my spirit upon the house of Israel, saith the Lord God.
—Ezek. 39:21, 22, 28, 29.

By application of one or more of these rules, the time of almost any prophecy may be determined. The amazing thing will be found to be how much prophecy relates to "the time of the end."

In prophecy it is necessary to split hairs; even minor errors must be corrected because they grow. When we are dealing with doctrinal differences, there is usually some truth on both sides, and the differences remain about the same through the years. But in prophecy, one conclusion becomes the basis for another; so a small error, unimportant in itself, grows until the departure from truth becomes so great as to amount almost to a false doctrine.

The only secret event is the Resurrection. The time of the return of Christ for His Church is a very closely guarded secret, and no times are given which would reveal it. (After the Resurrection, times are freely given.) The day and hour of the Resurrection is secret, but signs are numerous. To the believing Church, Jesus will *not* come as a thief in the night, for "ye, brethren, are not in darkness, that that day should overtake you as a thief" (I Thess. 5:4). Of course the world of that day will know little of the Bible, so that the return of Christ in glory *will* overtake *the world* as a thief in the night.

The Resurrection will also take Satan by surprise, but not so the return of Christ in glory. Satan will know of the near approach of that event and will know when to marshal his armies around Jerusalem. "Woe to the inhabiters of the earth and of the sea! for the devil is come down unto you, having great wrath, because *he knoweth* that he hath but a short time" (Rev. 12:12). The Church is very much involved in the Resurrection; the Jews as a nation are not.

TIMES SET FOR ISRAEL

Before the Rapture, times are *never* set for the Church, but times are *always* set for Israel. The Israelites have never been outside their land except a time has been set for their return. For instance, long before each event took place, Israel's exodus from Egypt, her 70 years' captivity in Babylon, as well as her 2520 years of world-wide dispersion among the nations were exactly foretold.

430 Years—Bondage in Egypt

Before the Israelites ever saw Egypt, their exodus from Egypt, including the date, had been foretold; indeed it was foretold before there were any Israelites. Even before the birth of Isaac, God told Abraham about the bondage, the return, and exactly how long it would be. This is told in Genesis 15:12–16:

> When the sun was going down, a deep sleep fell upon Abram; and, lo, an horror of great darkness fell upon him. And he said unto Abram, Know of a surety that thy seed shall be a stranger in a land that is not theirs, and shall serve them; and *they shall afflict them four hundred years;* and also that nation, whom they shall serve, will I judge: and afterward shall they come out with great substance. And thou shalt go to thy fathers in peace; thou shalt be buried in a good old age. But *in the fourth generation* they shall come hither again: for the iniquity of the Amorites is not yet full.

A generation was then considered a hundred years. This was apparently 30 years after Abraham's entrance into the Promised Land. So the entire time from Abraham's entrance into Palestine to the Exodus was to be 430 years. This was not an approximate time, *but an exact date.*

> Now the sojourning of the children of Israel, who dwelt in Egypt, was four hundred and thirty years. And it came to pass *at the end of the four hundred and thirty years, even the selfsame day* it came to pass, that all the hosts of the Lord went out from the land of Egypt. —Ex. 12:40, 41.

70 Years Captivity in Babylon

The second time the Israelites were forced to leave their land is called the Captivity. This refers specifically to Judah, inasmuch as the ten northern tribes had been scattered over Assyria some time before the fall of Jerusalem. More than one invasion of Judah was required to complete the captivity, and so the captivity took place over a period of about twenty years. It was during this time that Jeremiah predicted that they would serve the king of Babylon 70 years and then return to their own land. The time of the return was set and announced before they went into captivity.

> Therefore thus saith the Lord of hosts; Because ye have not heard my words, behold, I will send and take all the families of the north, saith the Lord, and Nebuchadnezzar the king of Babylon, my servant, and will bring them against this land, and against the inhabitants thereof, and against all these nations round about, and will utterly destroy them, and make them an astonishment, and an hissing, and perpetual desolations.
>
> Moreover I will take from them the voice of mirth, and the voice of gladness, the voice of the bridegroom, and the voice of the bride, the sound of the millstones, and the light of the candle. And this whole land shall be a desolation, and an astonishment; and *these nations shall serve the king of Babylon seventy years.* —Jer. 25: 8–11.
>
> For thus saith the Lord, That *after seventy years* be accomplished at Babylon, I will visit you, and perform my good word toward you, in causing you to return to this place. —Jer. 29:10.

Although during Jeremiah's lifetime his warnings went unheeded, his prediction of a 70 years' captivity was taken very seriously. The sacred historian added it to the record of the Fall of Jerusalem.

> And them that had escaped from the sword carried he away to Babylon; where they were servants to him and his sons until the reign of the kingdom of Persia: to fulfill the word of the Lord by the mouth of Jeremiah, until the land had enjoyed her sabbaths: for as long as she lay desolate she kept sabbath, *to fulfill threescore and ten years.*
>
> Now in the first year of Cyrus king of Persia, that the word of the Lord spoken by the mouth of Jeremiah might be accomplished, the Lord stirred up the spirit of Cyrus king of Persia, that he made a proclamation throughout all his kingdom, and put it also in writing, saying, Thus saith Cyrus king of Persia, All the kingdoms of the earth hath the Lord God of heaven given me; and he hath charged me to build him an house in Jerusalem, which is in Judah. Who is there among you of all his people? The Lord his God be with him, and let him go up. —II Chron. 36:20–23.

Daniel was taken captive in one of the raids and lived in Babylon during the entire seventy years. He was a student of Jeremiah and when the seventy years were up, Daniel became very much concerned about what was going to happen, apparently reading into the prophecy much more than was there. As a result, the angel was sent to Daniel to inform him of a further period of 70 sevens of years that were yet to be accomplished before Israel could look for complete redemption.

> And he hath confirmed his words, which he spake against us, and against our judges that judged us, by bringing upon us a great evil: for under the whole heaven hath not been as it hath been done upon Jerusalem.
> —Dan. 9: 12.

Isaiah's prophecies were much more detailed, even calling Cyrus by name: "That saith of Cyrus, He is my shepherd, and shall perform all my pleasure: even saying to Jerusalem, Thou shalt be built; and to the temple, Thy foundation shall be laid" (Isa. 44:28).

Jeremiah's prophecy is the only one mentioned in connection with the return, although from the proclamation of Cyrus it is apparent that the controlling factor was the prophecy of Isaiah.

That which made Jeremiah's prophecy stand out so strongly in the minds of the leaders was the time element. The time element is the most powerful detail of any prophecy; therefore, the time element of all prophecy is of extreme importance.

The most successful and troublesome false religions of our day are those that started by setting dates. Even though they were wrong, the fact that they claimed to know a date gave them an advantage over all others. *In a false religion, honesty and consistency are not virtues;* nevertheless they serve to illustrate how these prophecies that reveal times have the greatest impact upon the minds of hearers. Those times that are hidden, we should not try to pry into; but those that are revealed, we should understand thoroughly, for "the secret things belong unto the Lord our God: but those things which are revealed belong unto us and to our children for ever" (Deut. 29:29).

2520 Years Worldwide Dispersion

Both Daniel and Ezekiel foretold the number of years the Jews would be scattered among the nations: Daniel has a period of 490 years, divided into three parts (see Daniel Chapter 9); Ezekiel has two periods, one of 390 years and one of 40 years, making a total of 430 years.

The Qumran Commentaries (Dead Sea Scrolls) attempt an explanation of these figures. Although they rightly supposed that the length of the Dispersion was forecast in these prophecies, they fell into the common error of trying to make

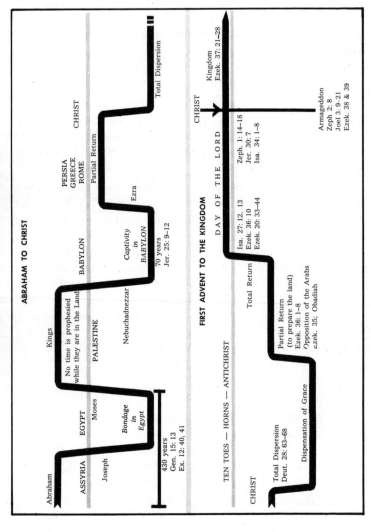

PROPHECY IN THE HISTORY OF ISRAEL

ABRAHAM TO CHRIST

Abraham

ASSYRIA   EGYPT
          Moses
Joseph

Bondage
in
Egypt

430 years
Gen. 15: 13
Ex. 12: 40, 41

Kings

No time is prophesied
while they are in the Land

PALESTINE

Nebuchadnezzar

BABYLON

Captivity
in
BABYLON

70 years
Jer. 25: 9-12

Ezra

PERSIA
GREECE
ROME

CHRIST

Partial Return

Total Dispersion

FIRST ADVENT TO THE KINGDOM

CHRIST

Total Dispersion
Deut. 28: 63-68

Dispensation of Grace

TEN TOES — HORNS — ANTICHRIST

Partial Return
(to prepare the land)
Ezek. 36: 1-8
Opposition of the Arabs
Ezek. 35; Obadiah

Total Return

Isa. 27: 12, 13
Ezek. 36: 10
Ezek. 20: 33-44

DAY OF THE LORD

CHRIST

Zeph. 1: 14-18
Jer. 30: 7
Isa. 34: 1-8

Kingdom
Ezek. 37: 21-28

Armageddon
Zeph 2: 8
Joel 3: 9-21
Ezek. 38 & 39

all prophecy culminate in their time. They tried to make the 430 years fit into the 490-year period and treated them as a re-interpretation of Jeremiah's seventy years.

However, the seventy years was an exact time. At the end of that period of captivity in Babylon, Palestine again became a Jewish homeland, and all who so desired could return. The prophecy of the 70 years' captivity was *literally* fulfilled by their return, and was recorded by Ezra and by Nehemiah.

But the return after the Babylonian Captivity was only *a partial return*, for many of the Jews remained in Babylon. After that time, Palestine never became independent. Throughout the years it was always a captive country so that the Jews never again had a reigning king. Successively, Palestine was dominated by Persia, by Greece, by Syria, and by Rome. Finally, the Jews were scattered once more among all countries, where they have remained until this day. For the first time in over 2500 years, there is today an independent Jewish state in Palestine.

Whenever the Israelites have been outside their land, times were always set for their return. But in the case of the return of the captives, there is a complication. In 536 B.C. some of them went back, and history follows the returned Jews down through the advent and rejection of Christ to the promised kingdom. But there is also the story of the other dispersion, which has always existed since the Fall of Jerusalem (586 B.C.) and which became complete again in A.D. 70. Because there are *two* lines of history, there are also *two* lines of prophecy: one about the Jews that returned to Palestine about 536 B.C.; the other about the Jews that were scattered among the nations, were later joined by those from Palestine, and are yet to return to their land.

In the Scriptures, therefore, one line of prophecy follows the Jews who returned. This includes the rebuilding

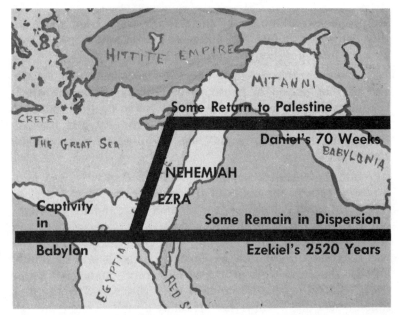

of Jerusalem and its wall, the rejection of Christ, the temporary lapse during the Dispensation of Grace and the experiences with Antichrist, and the end of iniquity. Daniel's prophecy of the 70 Weeks concerns these Jews who returned.

Ezekiel was told about those who did not return. How long their dispersion would be was revealed, but it was told in such a way that it would not influence its fulfillment nor point to the time of the Resurrection. Because of the fact that the return of the Jews is closely associated in time with the Resurrection, the time element *must* be somewhat veiled.

EZEKIEL'S DRAMATIZED PROPHECY

Ezekiel's account, then, of the number of years of dispersion is an acted-out prophecy which amounts almost to an enigma (Ezek. 4).

Then the spirit entered into me [Ezekiel]...and said unto me,...Thou also, son of man, take thee a tile, and lay it before thee, and pourtray upon it the city, even Jerusalem: and lay siege against it, and build a fort against it, and cast a mount against it; set the camp also against it, and set battering rams against it round about.

Moreover take thou unto thee an iron pan, and set it for a wall of iron between thee and the city: and set thy face against it, and it shall be besieged, and thou shalt lay siege against it. *This shall be a sign to the house of Israel.*

Lie thou also upon thy left side, and lay the iniquity of the house of Israel upon it: according to the number of the days that thou shalt lie upon it thou shalt bear their iniquity. For I have laid upon thee the years of their iniquity, according to the number of the days, *three hundred and ninety days:* so shalt thou bear the iniquity of the house of Israel.

And when thou hast accomplished them, lie again on thy right side, and thou shalt bear the iniquity of the house of Judah *forty days:* I have appointed thee each day for a year. Therefore thou shalt set thy face toward the siege of Jerusalem, and thine arm shall be uncovered, and thou shalt prophesy against it. And, behold, I will lay bands upon thee, and thou shalt not turn thee from one side to another, till thou hast ended the days of thy siege.—Ezek. 3: 24; 4: 1–8.

Ezekiel was told to take a tile and portray upon it the city of Jerusalem and lay siege against it by lying on his left side for 390 days. Each day was to represent one year of the iniquity of Israel. Next Ezekiel was told to lie on his right side for 40 days, each day for a year. Evidently these years were to begin with the siege of Jerusalem, for the Lord said, "Son of man, behold, I will break the staff of bread in Jerusalem: and they shall eat bread by weight and with care; and they shall drink water by measure and with astonishment: that they may want bread and water, and be astonished one with another, and consume away *for their iniquity*" (vs. 16, 17).

The purpose of this prophecy is stated frankly—to show how long the Jews will be scattered among the nations: "I have laid upon thee the years of their iniquity, according to the number of the days" (vs. 5). "I have appointed each day *for a year*" (vs. 6). "Even thus shall the children of Israel eat their defiled bread among the Gentiles, whither I will drive them" (vs. 13). This dramatized prophecy has only one announced purpose—to show that the length of time the Jews will be scattered among the nations is 390 years plus 40 years (vs. 5, 6).

But the iniquity and the dispersion of Israel and Judah did *not* end either in 390 years, nor in 40 more years. The fact is these figures from Ezekiel 4 simply do not point to any experience in the dispersion of the Jews. It is evident, therefore, that some other conditions or factors must be applied. Those conditions may be found in Leviticus 26:18: *"If ye will not yet for all this hearken unto me, then I will punish you seven times more for your sins."* Evidently there were to be two periods of punishment. The length of time of the first punishment is not given in Leviticus. (In Jeremiah and Daniel it is expressly given as seventy years, Jer. 29:10;* Dan. 9:2.§) The Lord does say that if *after that first period* they do *not* leave their sins and turn to God, *the balance of the punishment will be multiplied by seven.*

EZEKIEL'S 430 DAYS

Ezekiel laid siege to Jerusalem for a total of 430 days (390 plus 40), indicating 430 years of the determined punishment for Israel and Judah. If we subtract 70 from the 430 (they were punished in Babylon 70 years), we have a balance of 360 years. According to Leviticus 26:18, God told Moses that these 360 years would be multiplied by seven.

*For thus saith the Lord, That after seventy years be accomplished at Babylon I will visit you, and perform my good word toward you, in causing you to return to this place. —Jer. 29:10.

§ In the first year of his reign I Daniel understood by books the number of the years, whereof the word of the Lord came to Jeremiah the prophet, that he would accomplish seventy years in the desolations of Jerusalem. —Dan. 9:2.

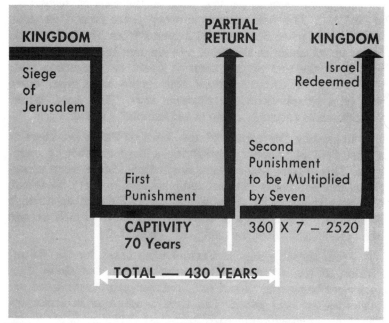

The number of years of world-wide dispersion for Israel is therefore 360 times 7 or 2520 years.

When, then, will the 2520 years of punishment for Israel end? All dates must be considered approximate, but they are near enough for our purpose. The captivity began about 606 B.C. and was complete about 586 B.C.—that is, the process of taking Palestine and the Jews captive took about twenty years. Seventy years from Nebuchadnezzar's first captivity in 606 B.C. saw the first return of the captives (536 B.C.), and seventy years from the final captivity of Nebuchadnezzar in 586 B.C. saw the final return (516 B.C.); therefore the return also took about twenty years. The prophecy of the 2520 years could start any time within that twenty-year period. It is so arranged that we cannot set actual dates in advance.

Assyrian records set the time of the Fall of Jerusalem at 586 B.C. The first return, seventy years from that date, would bring us to 516 B.C.; 2520 years from 516 B.C., would bring us to about A.D. 2004. We do not know what event will mark the end of this time. It could be something after the return of Christ. Before the return of Christ, there will be a temple built, for Malachi says, "The Lord, whom ye seek, shall suddenly come to his temple" (Mal. 3:1).

Regarding the return of the Jews to Palestine, there is a vast field of prophecy, involving a large number of countries. This return will require some time. Some very sensational developments (almost unbelievable, in fact) lie ahead. God was speaking of those events when He told us through Habakkuk, "I will work a work in your days, which ye will not believe, though it be told you" (Hab. 1:5).

From these figures in Ezekiel 4 no dates for the Resurrection or the return of Christ can be set. *But these 2520 years are beginning to run out, and the events scheduled are beginning to take place.* The time prophesied is about up. The Jews are beginning to return, and Palestine is returning to productivity. Two world wars have had only one tangible result—Palestine becoming what Ezekiel called it, *the center of the earth.*

This is sufficiently accurate for our purpose. For the full understanding, we will have to wait the event; but it will undoubtedly come, as did the going out of Egypt, *"on the selfsame day"* that the time is up.

This prophecy of the 2520 years concerns all Israel, those who returned and those who did not. It does not take note of the partial return under Ezra and Nehemiah, nor the partial return that is in progress now. Those partial returns are foretold in other places.

Study 2

DANIEL'S SEVENTY WEEKS
Daniel 9

DANIEL'S SEVENTY WEEKS
Daniel 9

Daniel, a student of prophecy, lived in Babylon during the entire seventy years of captivity from 606 B.C. to 536 B.C. The Fall of Babylon at the end of that time signaled to Daniel the end of the seventy years predicted by Jeremiah. Daniel, therefore, became very much concerned, for his people were in no condition for what he thought was going to happen. (Evidently Daniel thought that the restoration of Jerusalem foretold by Jeremiah was the Messianic Kingdom.)

Daniel therefore began to pray for the people. In answer to his prayer, God sent His angel to inform him that not seventy years but seventy "weeks" of years (seventy "sevens" of years) would have to pass before the final realization of his hopes could be looked for.

> Whiles I [Daniel] was speaking, and praying, and confessing my sin and the sin of my people Israel, and presenting my supplication before the Lord my God for the holy mountain of my God; yea, whiles I was speaking in prayer, even the man Gabriel, whom I had seen in the vision at the beginning, being caused to fly swiftly, touched me about the time of the evening oblation.
>
> And he informed me, and talked with me, and said, O Daniel, I am now come forth to give thee skill and understanding. At the beginning of thy supplications the commandment came forth, and I am come to show thee; for thou art greatly beloved: therefore understand the

matter, and consider the vision. *Seventy weeks are de-termined upon thy people and upon thy holy city.*
                                    —Dan. 9:20–24.

From the angel, Daniel learned that the seventy years of captivity would *not* end Israel's dispersion, neither would they bring in the Kingdom. These events would still be some time in the future. Several great events, revealed to Daniel at this time, were to happen first. Daniel had been right in supposing that the kingdom of Christ would be set up. He had been mistaken only as to the time. And so, it was the matter of time that the angel came to straighten out.

ACCOMPLISHMENTS OF THE 70 WEEKS

Seventy weeks are determined upon thy people and up-on thy holy city, to finish the transgression, and to make an end of sins, and to make reconciliation for iniquity, and to bring in everlasting righteousness, and to seal up the vision and prophecy, and to anoint the most Holy. —Dan. 9:24.

Concerning the seventy "weeks," it should be noted that in English we have names for certain periods of years, such as decade (10 years), century (100 years), and millennium (1,000 years); but we have no one word for "seven years," so it is translated "weeks," meaning weeks of years. Seventy "weeks" would mean 70 sevens, or 490 years. In this verse, it is the Jews and the city of Jerusalem that are involved in the period of seventy weeks.

Notice, then, the things to be accomplished in these 490 years:

To finish the transgression, and to make an end of sins.*
This whole phrase has various renderings, for both parts of

° At the beginning of paragraphs, each passage in boldface type refers back to the portion from Daniel set in boldface type at the beginning of each section.

it seem to be difficult to translate in such a way that they make sense. They refer back to what Daniel has just been saying in his prayer about his people: "We have sinned and have committed iniquity, and have done wickedly, and have rebelled, even by departing from thy precepts and from thy judgments" (Dan. 9:5). Within 70 weeks all this transgression was to be brought to an end.

The full meaning of the passage may be found in the books of Moses, for according to Daniel, "All Israel have transgressed . . . ; therefore the curse is poured upon us, and the oath that is written in the law of Moses the servant of God, because we have sinned against him" (vs. 11). Both the blessing and the curse are dramatically set forth in Deuteronomy 28:15: "It shall come to pass, if thou wilt *not* hearken unto the voice of the Lord thy God to observe to do all his commandments and his statutes which I command thee this day, that all these curses shall come upon thee, and overtake thee." In the most vivid detail, Moses then lists all the things that would happen (and have happened) to the Jews in the long years of their dispersion.

The 70 "weeks," then, were to bring an end to the cause of all their tribulation. "However, 'to finish the transgression' is not the same as 'to make an end of sins.' 'To finish the transgression' might better be translated 'to restrain the transgression.' "—*Pulpit Commentary.*

The first step in Israel's restoration is national repentance and turning to God.

It shall come to pass, when all these things are come upon thee, the blessing and the curse, which I have set before thee, and thou shalt call them to mind among all the nations, whither the Lord thy God hath driven thee, and *shalt return unto the Lord thy God,* and *shalt obey his voice* according to all that I command thee this day, thou and thy children, with all thine heart, and with all thy soul; that then the Lord thy God will turn thy captivity, and have compassion upon thee, and will return

and gather thee from all the nations, whither the Lord
thy God hath scattered thee. —Deut. 30:1–3.

This will not be the end of Israel's iniquity but only the
beginning of the end. Many in Israel will still deal with Antichrist. Armageddon is still ahead for them. To purge Israel
will take more than a national repentance. First there will
be a restraining of iniquity. The "end of sins" will come only
after the return of Christ when "they will look upon him
whom they have pierced." Then there will be complete re-
generation:

> I will take you from among the heathen, and gather
> you out of all countries, and will bring you into your own
> land. *Then* will I sprinkle clean water upon you, *and
> ye shall be clean:* from *all* your filthiness, and from *all*
> your idols, will I cleanse you. A *new heart* also will I give
> you, and *a new spirit* will I put within you: and I will
> take away the stony heart out of your flesh, and I will
> give you an heart of flesh.
> And I will put my spirit within you, and cause you
> to walk in my statutes, and ye shall keep my judgments,
> and do them. And ye shall dwell in the land that I gave
> to your fathers; and ye shall be my people, and I will be
> your God. —Ezek. 36:24–28.

To make reconciliation for iniquity. There is no word in
the Old Testament that could properly be translated reconciliation. In this verse the word *reconciliation* means atonement, "the offering of an atoning sacrifice." This is closely
associated with the next item, "*to bring in everlasting righteousness.*" It is significant that the other time this latter expression, everlasting righteousness, occurs in the Bible, it is
the righteousness of God: "Thy righteousness is an everlasting righteousness" (Ps. 119:142). Only in Christ is such a
righteousness found, for "it is not possible that the blood of
bulls and of goats should take away sins" (Heb. 10:4).

Concerning this verse in Daniel, the *Pulpit Commentary*
makes a very significant statement: "These two, 'atonement

for sin' and 'everlasting righteousness'—His atoning death, and the righteousness which He brings into the world—are found in Christ. It is true that when Daniel heard these words spoken by Gabriel, he might not have put any very distinct meaning on them. In that, Daniel was just like other prophets, for *the prophets did not know the meaning of their own prophecies.*"

Gabriel had come to Daniel to give him skill and understanding, yet Daniel could *not* have comprehended the full extent of the truths that Gabriel was uttering. Daniel knew about the righteousness of the law; but Gabriel was talking about a righteousness which was left for Christ to bring forth, a new righteousness which is not through the deeds of the law, wherein no flesh can be justified: "But now the righteousness of God *without the law* is manifested, being witnessed by the law and the prophets; even the righteousness of God which is *by faith of Jesus Christ* unto all and upon all them that believe" (Rom. 3:21, 22). This is the righteousness that Gabriel was talking about.

To seal up the vision and prophecy. "This does *not* refer to Jeremiah's prophecy, because his prophecy referred merely to the return from Babylon, and Daniel's words refer to a period which is to continue long after that. Though Jeremiah's prophecy was about to be verified, this new prophecy required 490 years ere it received its verification. It seems that some event, to happen nearly half a millennium after Daniel, is to prove the prophecy which God has given him to be true."—*Pulpit Commentary.*

To anoint the most Holy. "The most Holy" does *not* refer here to the holy of holies, which was never anointed, but to a person. Although anointing was used on rare occasions in reference to things, its usual application was the anointing of persons, as Aaron, Saul, David; for the Jews anointed kings. The Hebrew word *messiah* means "anointed." The reference, then, in the phrase "to anoint the most

Holy" is to Messiah, as will be seen in the very next verse
vs. 25.

This reference to anointing the most Holy has troubled
the commentators because Jesus was *not* officially anointed
king, but instead was rejected by the Jews. Daniel, however,
is referring not to the *first* advent but to the *second* advent
of Christ when He shall be "the Anointed" and shall be so
recognized by all Israel.

To accomplish these things, 70 weeks of years (490
years) are determined (vs. 24). A study of this prophecy indicates that the 70 weeks will run until the Second
Coming of Christ. Of course it is obvious, if we consider the
almost 2,000 years since Christ's birth, that this prophecy
must refer to far more than 490 years. Therefore, the prophecy is not explainable if the entire 490 years are to run con-
secutively without a break. But if you put the Dispensation
of Grace into this period as a parenthesis, then you can
figure out exactly 490 years until the events that take place
at the coming of Christ in glory.

DIVISIONS OF THE 70 WEEKS

**Know therefore and understand, that from the going
forth of the commandment to restore and to build Jerusalem
unto the Messiah the Prince shall be seven weeks, and threescore and two weeks: the street shall be built again, and the
wall, even in troublous times. —Dan. 9:25.**

Next the angel proceeds to break down the seventy
weeks into three smaller periods and indicates what each
one represents.

**From the going forth of the commandment to restore and to
build Jerusalem . . . : the street shall be built again, and the wall.**
The 490 years are to start with "the going forth of a decree
to restore and build Jerusalem." But the decree of King Cyrus

did not involve any rebuilding of the city. It simply states, "The Lord God of heaven...hath charged me to build him an house at Jerusalem" (Ezra 1:2). This clearly is not the decree intended. Likewise, when Ezra and his companions left Babylon and came to Jerusalem in the seventh year of Artaxerxes, still no command had been given to build again the walls of Jerusalem. (This was about 458 B.C.) But to Nehemiah, in the twentieth year of the reign of Artaxerxes, there was a command given to build the wall of Jerusalem. This brings us to about 445 B.C. It is possible that none of these is the command referred to by the angel but another

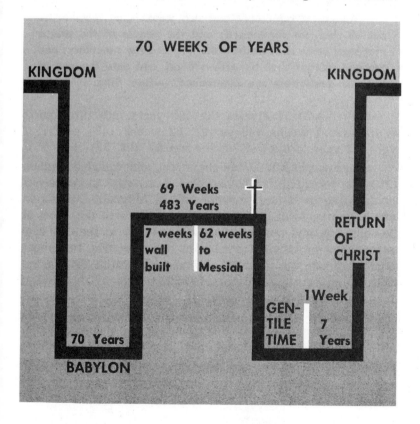

command from God that is not recorded. These dates serve only to show the general time.

Seven weeks, and threescore and two weeks. Sixty-nine weeks of years (483 years) from 458 B.C. would bring us to the year A.D. 25. If, however, we start with 445 B.C., it would bring us to A.D. 38. No one can fail to be struck with the fact that these dates are very near the most sacred date of all history—that of the crucifixion of our Lord.

THE END OF THE AGE

And after threescore and two weeks shall Messiah be cut off, but not for himself: and the people of the prince that shall come shall destroy the city and the sanctuary; and the end thereof shall be with a flood, and unto the end of the war desolations are determined. —Dan. 9:26.

Daniel 9:25–27 divides the 490 years into three parts as follows: 7 weeks (49 years); 62 weeks (434 years); 1 week (7 years), divided "in the midst" (vs. 27).

Seven weeks would see the street and wall built again. (This is recorded by Nehemiah.) *Sixty-two* more weeks would bring us to the "cutting off" of Messiah. Crucifixion was a Roman form of punishment unknown to the Jews of Daniel's day, and not specifically mentioned in the Old Testament. But crucifixion is referred to in the Old Testament in no uncertain terms, as, for instance, in Psalm 22. The rejection and "cutting off" of Messiah brings us to the end of the first 69 weeks (7 weeks and 62 weeks).

One week. The last division of the 490 years given here is one "week" (or 7 years). One "week" is yet to run, but the events of this week, the 70th week, did not take place immediately after the crucifixion. Between Daniel's 69th and 70th weeks, the Dispensation of Grace intervenes. The Jewish nation was side-tracked, and a new dispensation was begun, dominated by the Gentile Church, for "blindness in part is happened to Israel until the fulness of the Gentiles be come in" (Rom. 11:25).

Daniel's 70th week, then, is the last seven years before the return of Christ in glory. (In Revelation it corresponds to the seven last plagues, Rev. 15 and 16.)

This verse and the next one (vs. 27) are made more difficult because of the condition of the text and the difficulty of getting a good translation. The versions all differ; the general meaning, however, is clear.

Messiah shall be cut off but not for himself probably means that He was alone in His hour of trial. (From this point we skip to the end of the age.)

The prince that shall come is certainly Antichrist because Jesus referred to this passage and applied it to the end of the age (Matt. 24:15).* The destruction of the city and the sanctuary brings us to the very point of the coming of Christ.

And the end thereof shall be with a flood. This is thought not to be a literal flood but an overrunning of armies. But there will also be a flood, for there will be a very great earthquake so that the Mount of Olives will divide in the middle and a great valley will appear. This will open up an underground river which will flow out of Jerusalem in two directions and will flood much land (Zech. 14:8;§ Ezek. 47:1–5¶).

*When ye therefore shall see the abomination of desolation, spoken of by Daniel the prophet, stand in the holy place, (whoso readeth, let him understand).
—Matt. 24:15.

§ And it shall be in that day, that living waters shall go out from Jerusalem; half of them toward the former sea, and half of them toward the hinder sea; in summer and winter shall it be. —Zech. 14:8.

¶ Afterward he brought me again unto the door of the house; and, behold, waters issued out from under the threshold of the house eastward: for the forefront of the house stood toward the east, and the waters came down from under from the right side of the house, at the south side of the altar. Then brought he me out of the way of the gate northward, and led me about the way without unto the utter gate by the way that looketh eastward; and, behold, there ran out waters on the right side.
And when the man that had the line in his hand went forth eastward, he measured a thousand cubits, and he brought me through the waters; the waters were to the ancles. Again he measured a thousand, and brought me through the

THE COVENANT CONFIRMED

And he shall confirm the covenant with many for one week. —Dan. 9:27a.

He shall confirm the covenant is sometimes rendered, *he shall make a firm covenant.* But this has little support and does not make as much sense. "The covenant" is undoubtedly God's covenant with Israel concerning the land. It is this covenant that Antichrist confirms, thus trying to assume God's position as the protector of the Jew.

With many. Antichrist confirms God's covenant not with all the Jews, nor with Israel as a nation, but with "many." How much the nation is involved is not said. The charge is not made that Israel as a nation officially accepts the overtures of Antichrist. The *"many"* may perhaps be leaders and men in power. They, the many, are alone made responsible. For their disloyalty to God, the nation suffers.

Whatever may come from a "deal" with Antichrist, the benefits are short-lived, for in the middle of the "week," Israel will feel Antichrist's iron hand.

3½ YEARS TRIBULATION FOR ISRAEL

In the midst of the week he [Antichrist] shall cause the sacrifice and the oblation to cease, and for the overspreading of abominations he shall make it desolate. —Dan. 9:27b.

In the midst of the week. According to this statement in Daniel 9:27, the 70th week of 7 years will be divided "in the midst" into two halves of 3½ years each. This brings us to a study of the time element of 3½ years. Concerning the first

waters; the waters were to the knees. Again he measured a thousand, and brought me through; the waters were to the loins. Afterward he measured a thousand; and it was a river that I could not pass over: for the waters were risen, waters to swim in, a river that could not be passed over. —Ezek. 47:1–5.

half of this 70th week we have little to say, for little is said
about the Jews. Revelation has much to say about that time,
but Revelation concerns the nations, especially the kingdom
of the beast. Yet Palestine will not be immune from those
plagues, though they will not strike there with the same
intensity as they do in the rest of the world. Ezekiel says
that after the plagues are over, the nations converge on
Palestine for the expressed purpose of taking a great spoil:
"Art thou come to take a spoil? hast thou gathered thy
company to take a prey? to carry away silver and gold,
to take away cattle and goods, to take a great spoil?"
(Ezek. 38: 13).

The last half of the 70th week is "the time of Jacob's
trouble" (Jer. 30: 7). By this time, Antichrist has infiltrated
to the point of almost complete control. Such infiltration
would not have been possible if he had not been allowed to
"confirm the covenant." God will not prevent Antichrist
from entering Palestine; instead, God will use Jacob's trouble
for His own purpose, namely, the conversion of Israel: "He
shall be saved out of it" (Jer. 30: 7).

The pattern for "the time of Jacob's trouble" is the same
as for the tribulation for the saints. The length of time is
the same (3½ years). But the two events do *not* take place
simultaneously, for when the tribulation for Israel begins,
the tribulation of the saints, mentioned in Revelation 7, is
over. The purposes of the two tribulations are the same—to
bring people to God through Christ—but the method of tribulation will be adapted to the peculiar conditions. In both
cases there will be tribulation, accompanied by messengers
from heaven. But in the case of Israel, the result will be different. Today the gospel is effective on only a part of its
hearers; then, *all* Israel will be saved. (Rom. 11: 26).*

During the tribulation of the Jews, instead of messengers flying in the midst of heaven having the everlasting

* And so all Israel shall be saved: as it is written, There shall come out of
Sion the Deliverer, and shall turn ungodliness from Jacob. —Rom. 11:26.

gospel to preach (Rev. 14:6), there will be two witnesses sent from heaven, who will be easily recognizable because of their work. These two witnesses will duplicate the acts of Moses and Elijah and then will re-enact Jesus' death, resurrection, and ascension.

To the Jews the coming of these witnesses will be a sure sign, for they know that Elijah must first come. The disciples asked Jesus, "Why say the scribes that Elias must *first* come?" (Mark 9:11). The prophet Malachi said, "Behold, I will send you Elijah the prophet before the coming of the great and dreadful day of the Lord: and he shall turn the heart of the fathers to the children, and the heart of the children to the fathers, lest I come and smite the earth with a curse" (Mal. 4:5, 6).

The two witnesses will operate for 3½ years. Revelation 11:2, 3 says, "The holy city shall they tread under foot *forty and two months.* And I will give power unto my two witnesses, and they shall prophesy *a thousand two hundred and threescore days.*" During that time the forces of Antichrist will be "softening up" the Jews, preparatory to the great invasion called Armageddon. These 3½ years are the "times of the Gentiles" mentioned by Jesus.

> When ye shall see Jerusalem compassed with armies, then know that *the desolation thereof* is nigh. Then let them which are in Judæa flee to the mountains; let them which are in the midst of it depart out; and let not them that are in the countries enter thereinto.
>
> For these be the days of vengeance, that all things which are written may be fulfilled. But woe unto them that are with child, and to them that give suck, in those days! for there shall be great distress in the land, and wrath upon this people.
>
> And they shall fall by the edge of the sword, and shall be led away captive into all nations: and Jerusalem shall be trodden down of the Gentiles, until the times of the Gentiles be fulfilled. —Luke 21:20–24.

3½ YEARS TRIBULATION FOR THE SAINTS*

After the Resurrection, there will be a revival on earth. The outpouring of the Spirit, foretold by Joel (partially fulfilled at Pentecost), will result in a world-wide revival, the extent of which is recorded in Revelation 7—a multitude which no man could number of all nations and tribes. These will be the tribulation saints. Thus the outpouring of the Spirit will connect very definitely with the tribulation of the saints. There will be Jews saved, too, the same as today; but the revival will be largely among Gentiles.

This revival will have nothing to do with Daniel's 70th week and the 3½ years of tribulation for Israel. This revival is grace, not law, and will come *before* "the great and terrible day of the Lord." There will be three phases to the revival; first, the outpouring of the Spirit; second, signs in the heavens; third, "the day of the Lord," which, as in other places, is Daniel's 70th week.

> It shall come to pass afterward, that I will pour out my spirit upon all flesh; and your sons and your daughters shall prophesy, your old men shall dream dreams, your young men shall see visions: and also upon the servants and upon the handmaids in those days will I pour out my spirit.
> And I will shew wonders in the heavens and in the earth, blood, and fire, and pillars of smoke. The sun shall be turned into darkness, and the moon into blood, before *the great and terrible day of the Lord come.*
> And it shall come to pass, that whosoever shall call on the name of the Lord shall be delivered: for in mount Zion and in Jerusalem shall be deliverance, as the Lord hath said, and in the remnant whom the Lord shall call.
> —Joel 2:28–32.

Until the final Gentile revival is over, Daniel's 70th week can not start. This tribulation period is not the resumption of the old Dispensation of Law but the end of the dispensation of Grace. "Here are they that keep the commandments of

God, and the faith of Jesus" (Rev. 14:12). This will come *after* our gathering together unto Him. The reason there will be tribulation is that this is the time of the universal reign of Satan and the mark of the beast (Rev. 20:4, 5).

This revival and tribulation will come *before* Daniel's 70th week because those who are saved out of it are in the first resurrection.

> And I saw thrones, and they sat upon them, and judgment was given unto them: and I saw the souls of them that were beheaded for the witness of Jesus, and for the word of God, and which had not worshipped the beast, neither his image, neither had received his mark upon their foreheads, or in their hands; and they lived and reigned with Christ a thousand years.
> But the rest of the dead lived not again until the thousand years were finished. This is the first resurrection. —Rev. 20:4, 5.

Here we run into some modern teaching which, though almost universally accepted, cannot be supported by Scripture. Where does it say in the Bible that the Dispensation of Grace will end with the Rapture? Actually, the only place it could end is with the first resurrection; but *the tribulation saints will be in the first resurrection.*

In the Olivet Discourse Jesus called this tribulation of the saints "the beginning of sorrows," and He included it in the preaching of the gospel to all nations: "This gospel of the kingdom shall be preached in all the world for a witness unto all nations; and then shall the end [of the dispensation] come" (Matt. 24:14).

Jesus was talking here in His Olivet Discourse about the end of the age. The question He was answering was this: "What shall be the sign ... of the end of the world [or dispensation]?" (Matt. 24:3). When Jesus replied, "The end is not yet" (vs. 6), He meant the end of the age is not yet. Then He went on to tell what will happen in the end of the age. The two principal items will be the preaching of the gospel to all nations and the persecution of the tribulation saints. This preaching of the gospel will be accompanied by war, famine, pestilence, and earthquakes. But out of all this tribulation will come the great multitude of saved from every kindred, tongue, people, and nation.

This means that the Dispensation of Grace will not end at the Rapture, and that Daniel's 70th week will not begin at the Rapture. But then, where does the Bible say that the 70th week will begin with the Rapture? Any teaching that cannot be proved from Scripture is expendable.

A more logical as well as Scriptural place to begin Daniel's 70th week of law is *after* the first resurrection is complete, that is, after the resurrection of the tribulation saints. Of course this puts more than seven years between the Rapture and the return of Christ. But again, where does the Bible say anything about that time being just seven years? That idea has been added to the Scriptures without warrant.

It is not without significance that in the New Testament the first time the twelve tribes are named is in the same chapter as the resurrection of the tribulation saints. These 144,000 Israelites will not be raised with the other saved ones because they will not be killed. They will still be here, so they will be sealed and become the firstfruits of the coming kingdom. All this will happen at the close of the Dispensation of Grace and just as Daniel's 70th week is about to begin. In this way all the Scriptures fit together. But to try to put the tribulation of the saints in the last half of Daniel's 70th week throws the whole subject into such confusion that there is no hope of ever getting at the truth.

The tribulation saints will be a part of the Church (they are the seed of the woman, Rev. 12); they will be among those who live and reign with Christ a thousand years; they will come out of the Dispensation of Grace. The tribulation saints will have nothing to do with Israel, the two witnesses, the siege of Jerusalem, or any of the events of the last 3½ years. They will be in heaven before the seven last plagues.

On the other hand, during the last 3½ years, the attention of the whole world will be centered on Jerusalem, because all armies will be gathering there. Jerusalem will be the scene of the grand climax of the ages. This will not be the time of revival, of persecution (except for Israel), or of the worship of the image, for when the 3½ years begin, these things will be past. In those days Israel will be the focal point. The great battle of Armageddon will be at hand.

Thus the time of great revival and of persecution by Antichrist will come immediately *after* the Resurrection. The catching up of so many will, in itself, make a great impact on the world. Then will follow the battle for the hearts and minds of men: Satan, with his signs, his mark, and his persecution; God, with His mighty works in the heavens and in the hearts of men, and with His messengers flying through the sky with the everlasting gospel.

When that phase is over, all those believers whom Satan will kill will be raised, the 144,000 Israelites will be sealed, and the Dispensation of Grace, which began at Pentecost with an outpouring of the Spirit, will be over. (Joel's prophecy was not all fulfilled at Pentecost; therefore, it *must* be fulfilled *before* the dispensation is ended.)

We therefore can distinguish three periods of time between our gathering together and the return of Christ: two are in Daniel's 70th week; one comes *before* Daniel's 70th week.

What is the length of this first period, the period of the tribulation of the saints with which we are concerned now? Daniel mentions the years of the tribulation saints in Daniel 7:25.

> He shall speak great words against the most High, and shall wear out the saints of the most High, and think to change times and laws: and they shall be given

into his hand until *a time and times and the dividing of time.*

Daniel says the period of the tribulation of the saints is "a time and times and the dividing of times." This period is also referred to as 42 months, as 1260 days, as well as by the figurative expression—time, times, and half a time ("dividing of time"). All these expressions mean 3½ years.

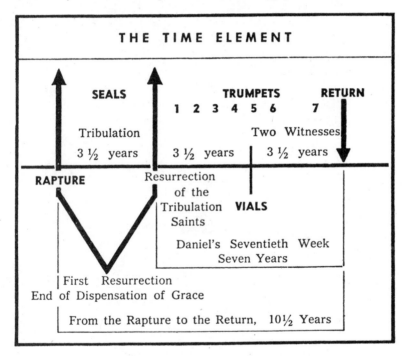

In conclusion, the Bible does not confuse Israel and the Church. The tribulation of the saints ends before the tribulation of the Jews begins. Tribulation is not a name for a definite period of time, but an experience that can come any time, or that can come to different people at different times. Jacob's Trouble is a time of tribulation for

Israel and has no connection with the Church. It should not be confused with the period of great tribulation that will come upon the saints saved after the Rapture, which brings this dispensation to an end. Daniel's 70th week comes *after* the Dispensation of Grace, not *during* it. Therefore, the time between the Rapture and the return of Christ is not 7 years, but 10½ years—3½ years plus 7 years. This puts everything in its place.

DANIEL'S FIRST VISION OF WORLD-EMPIRE

PANORAMA OF HISTORY
Daniel 2

PANORAMA OF HISTORY
Daniel 2

King Nebuchadnezzar is one of the greatest names in history, and his empire extended over the known world. Its capital, Babylon, was situated on the Euphrates River, and in its day was one of the largest and most beautiful cities in the world. In the time of King Nebuchadnezzar (after the Fall of Nineveh), Babylon was improved in magnificent style and at that time attained its greatest glory.

The great world-empires mentioned by Daniel did not all cover exactly the same territory. The movement of empires was from east to west, each succeeding empire extending its domains farther toward the setting sun. But there was one piece of land which was in all the world-empires—the land of Palestine. In fact, if all the land of the empires was put on one map, Palestine would be in the center. By degrees Palestine fell into the hands of Babylon. In one of the last raids, Daniel and his companions were taken captive but, because of their royal blood and good appearance, were selected to wait upon the king.

King Nebuchadnezzar's dream, as given in Daniel Chapter 2, was so unusual and startling that it made a great impression on the king. Yet he could not remember it. The scene in his palace is very striking: Excited and sleepless, the king calls out to his attendants to summon to his presence all the wise men in the capital of his empire, and demands an

explanation of his dream. This was not an unusual thing.
Nebuchadnezazr reasons that if the wise men have supernatural knowledge, they ought to be able both to reconstruct
and to interpret the dream; in fact, he makes *that* a test of
their knowledge and ability. But all the wise men of Babylon can *not* tell the king his dream and say such knowledge
belongs to the gods "whose dwelling was not with flesh."
Then in anger, the king commands that all Babylon's wise
men be killed. Although, at the king's urgent command,
Daniel is not summoned with these men (probably because
of his youth and incomplete training), he *is* considered one
of the wise men and so was included among those who were
to die. But Daniel asks the king for extended time. This is
granted, so Daniel and his companions hold a prayer meet-
ing. That night the dream and its meaning are revealed to
Daniel. Then Daniel prays again, and his prayer is preserved
for us:

> Blessed be the name of God for ever and ever:
> for wisdom and might are his: and he changeth the
> times and seasons; he removeth kings, and setteth up
> kings: he giveth wisdom unto the wise, and knowledge
> to them that know understanding:
> He revealeth the deep and secret things: he knoweth
> what is in the darkness, and the light dwelleth with
> him. I thank thee, and praise thee, O thou God of my
> fathers, who hast given me wisdom and might, and
> hast made known unto me now what we desired of thee:
> for thou hast now made known unto us the king's
> matter. —Dan. 2:20–23.

In this prayer Daniel expressed the substance of the dream:
It is God who changes times and seasons; it is God who re-
moves and sets up kings; it is God who reveals the secret
things of the future.

Next, Daniel went to Arioch, the king's captain, and declared that he was ready to tell the dream and the interpretation. Arioch was very human, took all the credit to himself,

and went at once to the king and said, "I have found a man that will make known to the king the interpretation." Unlike Arioch, when Daniel was ushered into the presence of the king, he was careful to give God all the glory. But he also took advantage of the situation to tell the king about the true God, the God whom Nebuchadnezzar finally came to know and honor, for he explained, *"There is a God in heaven that revealeth secrets, and maketh known to the king Nebuchadnezzar what shall be in the latter days."*

The King's Dream

Thou, O king, sawest, and behold a great image. This great image, whose brightness was excellent, stood before thee; and the form thereof was terrible. This image's head was of fine gold, his breast and his arms of silver, his belly and his thighs of brass, his legs of iron, his feet part of iron and part of clay.

Thou sawest till that a stone was cut out without hands, which smote the image upon his feet that were of iron and clay, and brake them to pieces.

Then was the iron, the clay, the brass, the silver, and the gold, broken to pieces together, and became like the chaff of the summer threshingfloors; and the wind carried them away, that no place was found for them: and the stone that smote the image became a great mountain, and filled the whole earth. —Dan. 2:31-35.

Thou, O king, sawest, and behold a great image. In the dream, the king had seen a great image, brilliant and terrible in appearance. The image's head was of fine gold, its breast and arms were of silver, its belly and thighs of brass, its legs of iron, and its feet partly of iron and partly of clay. While the king was considering the image, he saw a stone, cut out by an unseen power, come like a great falling star and strike the image on its feet. Immediately the whole image

DANIEL'S IMAGE

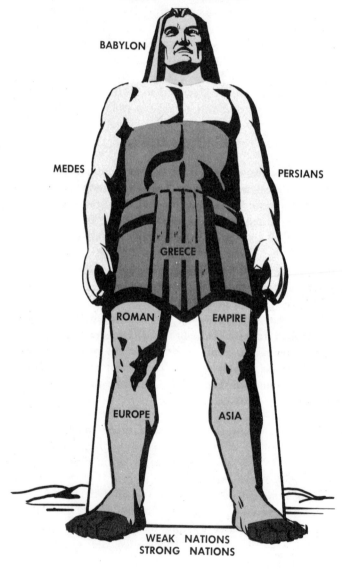

crumbled, the gold, silver, brass, iron, and clay became dust, and the wind blew all of it away. Then the stone began to grow till it took the place of the image and finally became a great mountain filling the whole earth. No wonder when King Nebuchadnezzar dreamed this dream, "his spirit was troubled and his sleep brake from him" (2:1).

It is not surprising that the king should dream about an image, for the Babylonians worshipped images. But this image was different. Its tremendous size, its gold, shining in the sun, its great silver arms, and its sturdy iron legs—all these gave the impression of strength and stability. Surely here was an image worth worshipping, something that would stand forever.

Let us look at the image a little more closely. Four metals appear (gold, silver, brass and iron), decreasing in value but increasing in strength from head to toe. Only in the toes do we find an element of weakness, an element which is not another metal but miry clay.

The gold is in *one* piece (the image's head); the silver is divided into *two* arms; the brass is *one* piece (belly and thighs); the iron is divided, first into *two* parts (two legs), and then into *ten* parts (ten toes). Only in the ten toes on which the image stood does any suggestion of weakness come. Baked in the sun, clay is brittle, so that in the toes the mixing the clay with the iron gives the whole structure an insecure foundation.

"God in heaven . . . maketh known to the king Nebuchadnezzar what shall be *in the latter days*" (vs. 28). The image of Nebuchadnezzar was symbolic of the world's political future; and so, according to Daniel, the image was meant to show what would take place in *the latter days*. Such Bible expressions as "the latter days," "that day," "the day of the Lord," etc., refer to the end of an age. They usually mean the age ending with the Second Coming of Christ.

It is in harmony with the whole nature of prophecy that there should be a summary of political events. Originally man was given dominion, so that human governments are said to be divinely established. The Coming of Christ, therefore, is a political event. *He* will depose kings and set up kings, as Daniel said. The Kingdom of God supersedes the kingdoms of the world.

In this vision, Daniel first shows the impressive structure of human government, and then later its inherent weakness (whenever it stands opposed to the divine program). Daniel's image presents the following items:

Head—*of gold*
Breast and arms—*of silver*
Belly and thighs—*of brass*
Legs—*of iron*
Feet—*of iron and clay*

The image is magnificent, brilliant and terrible. But there is a weakness. The only element of weakness—the clay—is in the feet on which the image stands. That is a most vital place—the very foundation. To crumble the whole image, the stone needs to strike not the head nor the trunk but only the feet.

The world-empires of Daniel, then, represent all human government, and so Daniel said to Nebuchadnezzar, "Wheresoever the children of men dwell . . . hath he [God] given into thine hand, and hath made thee ruler over them all." Here in this image, we have God's estimate of human government in general, as represented by the great world-empires.

THE FIRST WORLD-EMPIRE—BABYLON

Thou, O king, art a king of kings: for the God of heaven hath given thee a kingdom, power, and strength, and glory. And wheresoever the children of men dwell, the beasts of the field and the fowls of the heaven hath he given into thine hand, and hath made thee ruler over them all. Thou art this head of gold. —Dan. 2:37, 38.

Daniel told the king his dream and then proceeded to tell the interpretation, saying, "There is a God in heaven that revealeth secrets, and maketh known to the king Nebuchadnezzar *what shall be in the latter days.*"

Daniel's interpretation that *"thou . . . art a king of kings"* would please the proud king, and we can imagine that he nodded his head in ready assent. (To the credit of Nebuchadnezzar, it must be stated that when the interpretation was less favorable, he did not condemn Daniel.)

So far the interpretation was entirely reasonable and agreeable to the king. However, the next statement must have been astounding both to Daniel and to the king: "After thee shall arise another kingdom inferior to thee." The head of gold represented Nebuchadnezzar as the head of the empire. "*After* thee" does not mean Nebuchadnezzar was dead and his successor was on the throne. "After thee" means that following the entire Babylonian Empire another empire would rise. Daniel was telling Nebuchadnezzar that a kingdom inferior to Babylon would conquer Babylon.

Daniel could not have made a more improbable prophecy than this, for Babylon was considered impregnable. The city was built in the form of a square, each side of which was fourteen miles long. A wall, fifty-six miles in circumference, enclosed the city. The *Encyclopedia Britannica* says, "According to Herodotus, the height of the walls was 335 feet, and their width 85 feet."

A moat filled with water surrounded the wall. Some idea of the size and depth of this moat can be obtained from the fact that the clay from which the brick in the wall was made was taken from this moat.

The river Euphrates ran through the middle of the city, dividing it into two parts. The wall extended down both sides of the river, so the river could not be used by an enemy to enter the city. Babylon contained fifty streets, twenty-five running each way. Where the river intersected these streets, there were gates through the walls, gates of iron with brazen lintels and posts. Ferry boats plied between landing places at the gates, and at least one drawbridge joined the two parts of the city. At each end of the bridge was a palace. The great palace of Nebuchadnezzar was on the eastern side.

Babylon was self-supporting, so it could not be starved out by siege. This, then, is the city that Daniel said would fall before a weaker force. This prophecy, however, was not fulfilled in Nebuchadnezzar's time but took place about seventy years later when King Belshazzar reigned over Babylon. At that time a Persian named Cyrus had begun to conquer one land after another until he had made himself master of all the world outside of Babylon.

THE SECOND WORLD-EMPIRE—MEDO-PERSIA

And after thee shall arise another kingdom inferior to thee.... —Dan. 2:39a.

Cyrus the Persian had formed an alliance with the Medes, and his empire was known as the kingdom of the Medes and Persians. Then Cyrus and his army laid siege to Babylon and for years threatened the city. He dug a big lake and arranged to turn the course of the river Euphrates and dry up the river bed in case there should come a night when the gates along the river would not be shut. If Cyrus had known about the prophecy of Isaiah, spoken about 150 years before, he would have known for sure that the gates would not be shut, for in Isaiah we read,

> I am the Lord...that saith to Jerusalem, Thou shalt be inhabited; and to the cities of Judah, Ye shall be built, and I will raise up the decayed places thereof; ...That saith of Cyrus, He is my shepherd, and shall perform all my pleasure: even saying to Jerusalem, Thou shalt be built; and to the temple, Thy foundation shall be laid.
>
> Thus saith the Lord to his anointed, to Cyrus, whose right hand I have holden, to subdue nations before him; and I will loose the loins of kings, *to open before him the two-leaved gates; and the gates shall not be shut;* I will go before thee, and make the crooked places straight: I will break in pieces the gates of brass and cut in sunder the bars of iron:
>
> And I will give thee the treasures of darkness, and hidden riches of secret places, that thou mayest know that I, the Lord, which call thee by thy name, am the God of Israel. For Jacob my servant's sake, and Israel mine elect, I have even called thee by thy name: I have surnamed thee, though thou hast not known me.
>
> —Isa. 44:24, 26, 28; 45:1–4.

The Fall of Babylon

The story of the fall of Babylon is found in Daniel Chapter 5. Belshazzar, the king, made a great feast for a

One of the gates of Babylon still well preserved

thousand of his lords, and drank more than any of them. The whole city was celebrating. During the banquet, King Belshazzar called for the sacred vessels that had been taken out of the temple to Babylon by Nebuchadnezzar. As King Belshazzar and his guests were about to drink out of them, he saw a Hand, writing on the wall. It frightened and sobered him. Then followed the usual process of calling the wise men to read the writing. When they all failed, the king made so much commotion that the queen came into the hall, and fearing that the king would do some rash thing, suggested that Daniel be called.

Daniel was now an old man, close to ninety. It was nearly seventy years since, as a young man, he had predicted the fall of Babylon. During the reign of the wicked Belshazzar, he had been all but forgotten; but now a search was made for him, and he was found and brought into the banquet room.

In desperation, Belshazzar offered to make Daniel the third ruler of the land if he would read the writing and tell the meaning. (This promise was evidently kept, for when Cyrus took over the city, he found Daniel in charge and kept him in that position.)

First Daniel read the writing, "MENE, MENE, TEKEL, UPHARSIN"; then he gave the meaning: *"Mene—God hath numbered thy kingdom and finished it."* Seventy years had been determined upon Israel as the length of her captivity. Jeremiah had said, "This whole land shall be a desolation, and an astonishment: and these nations shall serve the king of Babylon seventy years" (Jer. 25:11). The seventy years were nearly complete. The numbering was finished. Cyrus "the anointed" was even now turning the course of the Euphrates into his man-made lake, and his army was standing ready to march into the city. In the midst of Babylon's celebrations, the Babylonians had forgotten to close the gates.

"Tekel—Thou art weighed in the balances and found wanting." God had weighed the gold of the image, representing Babylon and its king, and had found it wanting.

"Peres—Thy kingdom is divided and given to the Medes and Persians." Peres is the word used to explain Upharsin (meaning "divided"). Peres refers to Persia, which was the world-empire that was to follow Babylon. This second world-empire was a divided kingdom, made up of Medes and Persians. As the two arms of the image divided the silver, so

the great empire of Nebuchadnezzar was divided and given to the Medes and Persians. The first part of Daniel's prophecy had now been fulfilled.

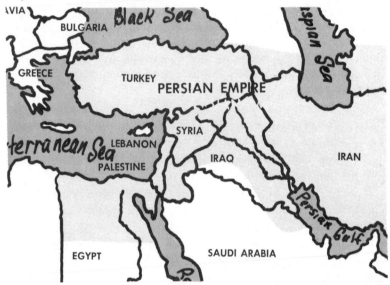

As we have already said, at the time this prophecy was given, it must have been astounding both to Daniel and to the king. But years later Daniel lived to see the Persian kingdom, "inferior to Babylon," conquer Babylon when God "loosed the loins of kings and opened before him the two-leaved gates" and let the enemy into Babylon in the time of Cyrus! A second and third world-empire followed Babylon in regular succession.

THE THIRD WORLD-EMPIRE—GREECE

And another third kingdom of brass, which shall bear rule over all the earth. —Dan. 2:39b.

The third world-empire was Greece, and came into existence when Alexander the Great conquered the world.

Just here not much is said about these empires, but other details are shown in future visions. (A characteristic of all prophecy is that details increase as we approach the end time.)

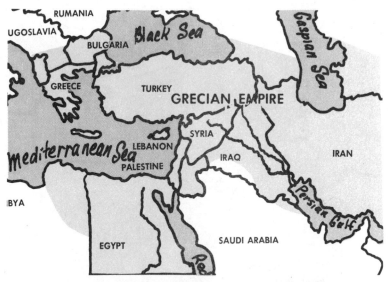

THE FOURTH WORLD-EMPIRE—ROMAN

And the fourth kingdom shall be strong as iron: forasmuch as iron breaketh in pieces and subdueth all things: and as iron that breaketh all these, shall it break in pieces and bruise.

And whereas thou sawest the feet and toes, part of potters' clay, and part of iron, the kingdom shall be divided; but there shall be in it of the strength of the iron, forasmuch as thou sawest the iron mixed with miry clay.

And as the toes of the feet were part of iron, and part of clay, so the kingdom shall be partly strong, and partly broken. And whereas thou sawest iron mixed with miry clay, they shall mingle themselves with the seed of men: but they

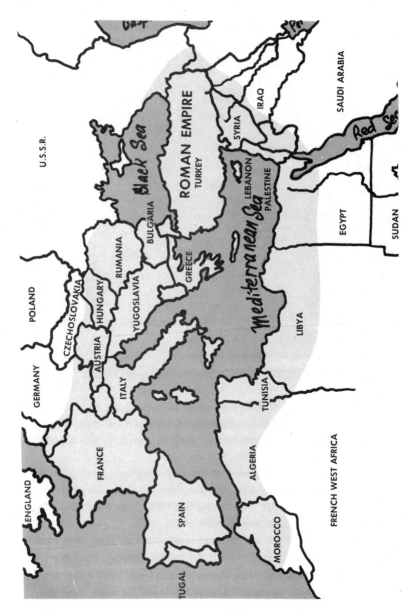

shall not cleave one to another, even as iron is not mixed with clay. —Dan. 2:40–43.

The fourth kingdom was the Roman Empire, which ruled the world with an iron hand. It destroyed Jerusalem in 70 A.D. and completed the dispersion of the Jews. The Roman Empire was divided into two parts, the East and West, corresponding to the two legs of the image.

The fourth kingdom shall be strong as iron. This does *not* mean that it would have a strong central government. The Roman Empire had a strong central government, but that feature was not pictured by this symbol. However, the Roman Empire was also a mighty empire, ruling conquered peoples with an iron hand, and so, the iron refers to the kind of power the empire exerted in the world and not to the form of government that exerted the power.

Forasmuch as iron breaketh in pieces and subdueth all things; and as iron that breaketh all these, shall it break in pieces and bruise. This is a remarkable, long-range prophecy. Daniel was saying in effect:

Babylon will fall and have a successor. It did—Persia.
Persia will fall and have a successor. It did—Greece.
Greece will fall and have a successor. It did—Rome.

This is exactly what happened. There were intervening wars, but in time Rome took over the reins of world-empire. (In prophecy, unimportant details are skipped over many times.)

The feet and toes part of potters' clay and part of iron. Here we are told something about these countries that were once a part of the Roman Empire. There will be a mixture. They will be like iron, and they will also be like clay. Clay is the non-metallic substance in the image. Clay is the only divisive material in the whole image. Clay weakens the whole structure, causes the empire to break up, and prevents it from coming back together again. Clay is the reason every attempt at a United States of Europe has failed.

It seems strange that any one should interpret the iron to mean strong central government (such as a monarchy or dictatorship) and the clay to mean democracy (popular rule). Yet that is the meaning often given to these symbols. But democracies have proven themselves to be just as strong as monarchies. The President of the United States is probably the most powerful man in the world, much more powerful than the king or queen of England. This is the important part of the prophecy, and more space is given to its explanation than to any other feature. When God goes to such lengths to explain a symbol, it is only reasonable that we should accept His explanation and not set up one of our own.

The kingdom shall be divided. Daniel declares that the fourth empire (Rome) would *not* fall before another power and would *not* have a successor. Instead, the Roman Empire would be *divided,* broken up into many nations, which in prophecy are called "kings." These nations remain intact until the end when "in the days of these kings the God of heaven shall set up a kingdom." The ten toes, then, represent the *dividing of the empire.* This is an important point. It will help in the interpretation of the more difficult visions to come. *The ten toes do not represent the revival or uniting of the empire.* The toes have already been divided and have now been in existence for 1500 years.

The Roman Empire, then, was divided into small nations. Some of these retained empire strength and thus throughout the years remained independent nations; others were less stable, for they had little of the iron and, at the insistence of stronger countries, were continually being broken up and having their boundaries changed. They are the clay countries.

There shall be in it of the strength of the iron. Iron is empire strength. This tells us something of the history of these countries: they will have some strength; they will remain until the coming of the Kingdom of God; they can *not* be dissolved nor brought to an end by absorption into some country outside the Roman Empire.

For 1500 years every attempt to conquer any of them has failed. Today we are faced with the most ambitious attempt to take over some of these countries since Genghis Khan in the thirteenth century. Russia has actually broken three toes off the image, having taken over totally Rumania, Bulgaria, and Hungary. The armies of these countries are being trained to fight Russia's battles. But it will not work; it cannot last; it is contrary to the prophecy. There can be no world peace while such a condition exists. World affairs will get worse until there is a focus on these three countries. They are the key to the future because they are prophetically out of place. Mark those countries well and watch them. God will break Russia, or Russia will break Daniel.

Let me repeat: It has been said that the iron represents strong or monarchical government, and clay represents democracies. This explanation does not satisfy the demands of the symbol. Daniel does not consider democracies. Iron is the metal that represents the empire and stands for empire strength. Clay is brittle and easily broken up. It is the element which divides the empire and allows it to break up into the various kingdoms represented by the ten toes.

And as the toes of the feet were part iron and part clay, so the kingdom shall be partly strong and partly broken (brittle). This is packing a lot of history into a small space, but it tells the story of these nations for the entire length of their existence. As the head of this great image represented the first world-empire to be considered, so the feet represent the present and final condition of world-empire. The feet, says Scripture, were "mixed with miry clay; nevertheless they had in them the strength of iron." This is a remarkable prophecy, especially in view of present-day conditions. The sign that the great image is about to stand again on toes of clay and that the final stage of Daniel's prophecy to Nebuchadnezzar will be fulfilled will be the rise of nations with ambitions for world-dominion.

They shall mingle themselves with the seed of men; but they shall not cleave one to another. For the sake of political alliance, rulers have intermarried, but this has never brought peace among them.

THE KINGDOM OF GOD—THE STONE

And in the days of these kings shall the God of heaven set up a kingdom, which shall never be destroyed: and the kingdom shall not be left to other people, but it shall break in pieces and consume all these kingdoms, and it shall stand for ever.

Forasmuch as thou sawest that the stone was cut out of the mountain without hands, and that it brake in pieces the iron, the brass, the clay, the silver, and the gold; the great God hath made known to the king what shall come to pass hereafter: and the dream is certain, and the interpretation thereof sure. —Dan. 2:44, 45.

In the days of these kings is an indication of time. It refers to the time when the Roman Empire will exist as a group of independent nations. These will delegate authority to the man whom the book of Revelation calls "the beast." Thus, after the Roman Empire, Daniel does not recognize any empire until the Kingdom of God comes. (Antichrist will reign, but his reign is brief and his kingdom unstable.)

"The days of these kings" may imply an even more specific time. It *could* mean the days when these kings are all powerful so far as world domination is concerned. Just as "the day of the Lord" refers to the time when the power of God is felt in the world, so "the days of these kings" may be the time of their great power. (In the vision of this chapter, Daniel does not tell *how* all this will come about; those details he gives later.)

We have now the following outline of history:

Parts of the Image and Materials	World-Empires
Head—gold	Babylon
Breast and arms—silver	Persia
Belly and thighs—brass	Greece
Legs—iron	Rome
Feet—iron and clay	Divided Empire

This image was a marvelous spectacle. Its great size and brilliance were terrifying. Its mammoth iron legs stood ready to crush everything in its way. This mighty symbol of world dominion, domineering, irresistible, without feeling, without mercy, seemed like an indestructible, eternal thing. No power on earth could match it. No voice could be raised against it. It stood like the tower of Babel, the symbol of human might.

Nevertheless, twice we are told that when the stone strikes the image, it breaks in pieces the gold, the silver, the brass, and the iron. When the stone strikes, the image is standing. But today, the gold, silver, and brass have all disappeared; only the iron and clay of the feet are left. If the stone should strike now, it could crumble only the toes. So, great things are going to happen in the Middle East; unheard-of changes are coming in Iran, Iraq, Syria, Arabia, Egypt, and Palestine. The world will again revolve around the Middle East. The world's greatest cities will be in some of those countries. When Christ comes, the image will be standing.

Thou sawest till that a stone was cut out without hands, which smote the image upon his feet that were of iron and clay, and brake them to pieces. Opposed to the mighty image was not even a metal but just a stone. A stone bears a closer relationship to clay than to any metal. The stone would be despised by those dictators who are represented by gold, silver, brass, or iron. The stone represents Him, who—despised and rejected of men—"is become the head stone of the corner" (Ps. 118:22).

The stone smote the image on the feet. The stone struck the image in its final form. The whole image turned to dust, and the wind blew it away. It should be noted that the image represents the governments of the nations and not all the people in those nations. The Lord will not destroy all the people who happen to be citizens or subjects of the nations in the final world-empire. It will be their armies that will be destroyed. It will be their governments that will be overthrown. All rulership of a purely human origin will cease. The kingdom will be the Lord's, and He will appoint His rulers.

The stone ... became a great mountain and filled the whole earth. A "mountain" represents a kingdom. After the defeat of the nations, the kingdom of God will be set up in Jerusalem and will spread over the whole earth.

> In the last days it shall come to pass, that the mountain of the house of the Lord shall be established in the top of the mountains, and it shall be exalted above the hills; and people shall flow unto it.
>
> And many nations shall come, and say, Come, and let us go up to the mountain of the Lord, and to the house of the God of Jacob; and he will teach us of his ways, and we will walk in his paths: for the law shall go forth of Zion, and the word of the Lord from Jerusalem.
>
> And he shall judge among many people, and rebuke strong nations afar off; and they shall beat their swords into plowshares, and their spears into pruninghooks: nation shall not lift up a sword against nation, neither shall they learn war any more.

But they shall sit every man under his vine and under his fig tree; and none shall make them afraid: for the mouth of the Lord of hosts hath spoken it. —Mic. 4: 1–4.

The dream is certain, and the interpretation thereof sure (vs. 45). Since these words were spoken, 2500 years have gone by, and we can now test their accuracy. It is a thrilling experience to think back over these years and realize how true Daniel's words are! How much has happened! How many times the prophecy could have been upset! Yet every detail has come true.

Daniel lived to see the first prediction happen, for he was there when Babylon fell to the Persians, and he himself became a ruler in the new Persian empire. When Jerusalem was rebuilt, Daniel's prophecies must have been carried there too, but for many years they were all but forgotten—though in the Olivet Discourse (Luke 21) Jesus referred to them.

The Persian Empire lasted about two hundred years; then Alexander the Great of Greece, in a brilliant series of battles, subjugated the entire Persian Empire and became master of the known world. Although brief as to time, Alexander's rule produced vast results in the world. After his death, his generals formed a compact for the government of the empire, but this was soon broken. In its place four kingdoms arose, roughly speaking, toward Asia, Africa, Syria, and Europe. Only the European section grew into another great empire. Eventually, the Roman Empire developed from there.

Then there came a time of shifting of world power. For a time Egypt was supreme. Then Syria dominated the scene. During the Syrian supremacy, the Jews of Palestine were subjected to severe persecution under Antiochus Epiphanes, and the Maccabean revolt brought some measure of independence.

It was not until about 60 B.C. that Roman supremacy began. The Roman Empire was the most highly organized and the longest in duration of any empire in ancient history. It lasted until 476 A.D., and even then the eastern division remained for many centuries with almost unbroken power. Daniel saw all this in his various visions and recorded it with the accuracy of a historian.

Now we come to the end of the long story. For nearly 1500 years—an incredibly long time as nations go—the toes of the image have existed. During all this time two characteristics have prevailed. As nations, the ten toes could not be wiped out or absorbed into outside countries, nor could they be united into one empire again. Both of these things have been tried over and over again.

Today we are entering a time of crisis for these ten toes. One great all-powerful nation has already "taken" three of these countries and now stands poised to destroy the others. This is not only a world crisis; it is a prophetic crisis. Russia can *not* succeed and the prophecy remain. It will be Russia, not the prophecy, that will suffer, for *"the dream is certain, and the interpretation sure."* All the prophecy of Daniel has been fulfilled except one item for which the world has been waiting ever since the toes came into being: "In the days of these kings *shall the God of heaven set up a kingdom"* (vs. 44).

Study 4

DANIEL'S SECOND VISION
OF WORLD-EMPIRE

THE FOUR BEASTS
Daniel 7:1-14

THE FOUR BEASTS
Daniel 7:1-14

On four different occasions Daniel was given revelations concerning the political future of the world. None of these visions are complete in themselves. Each omits important details found in the others. In the main, they progress from the general to the particular—that is, from the rise and fall of world-empires to the one individual who will represent world-empire in the last days prior to the Second Coming of Christ. Taken as one revelation, the four visions begin with world-empires in general and then end with the person and acts of Antichrist, the head of the last phase of its history. In each succeeding vision, the added details are mostly at the latter end of the vision and concern the last days of this age.

Because *four* is the world number, we should expect to find *four* visions about world-empires. But there are other reasons for *four* visions. Symbols have their limitations. One symbol cannot express all the factors in a series of events. Ten toes might symbolize the nations that grew out of the Roman Empire, but to show the reunion of those nations under one head, symbols of a different nature would be required. The great image served well enough to show the rise and fall of world-empires and the method of establishing the kingdom of God in the world, but the image is inadequate to reveal the intricate details of the last days. Thus the main purpose of this second vision is to add details to the general outline already revealed.

In Chapter 7 by the use of animals as symbols, it is possible to show many details not included in the image of Daniel 2. Three of the animals are named, but do not to any extent resemble the animals named. They are merely symbols. Great liberty is taken in the description of their appearance.

How God Writes History

Daniel spake and said, I saw in my vision by night, and behold, the four winds of the heaven strove upon the great sea. And four great beasts came up from the sea, diverse one from another. —Dan. 7:2, 3.

Four beasts came up from the sea. The sea, in Scriptural symbolism, represents humanity, world-wide: "He saith unto me, *The waters* which thou sawest, where the whore sitteth, *are peoples, and multitudes, and nations and tongues*" (Rev. 17:15).

It should be remembered that in the book of Daniel we are seeing how God writes history—world history. The story of the nations is told not by the long process of delineating the history of every nation that was to rise, but rather by the use of typical empires. For instance, the third kingdom of brass was said "to bear rule over all the earth" (2:39). Brass was merely a symbol of Greece; and Greece, in turn, was a type of man's rule over all the earth. These typical empires were so situated that their history is sufficient for all empires. The whole history of the earth is seen through them. In the end time, the whole world will again revolve around these prophetic lands.

THE FIRST BEAST—A LION

The first was like a lion, and had eagle's wings: I beheld till the wings thereof were plucked, and it was lifted up

from the earth, and made to stand upon the feet as a man, and a man's heart was given to it. —Dan. 7:4.

The first beast was like a lion. The same ground that was covered by the image of Nebuchadnezzar is covered in this series of visions, but more hurriedly. Only four verses are given to the four empires of the past. All the rest of the chapter of twenty-eight verses is devoted to the man we call Antichrist and the final scenes of this age in which he figures. One purpose of these four preliminary verses is to set the stage for the final events—that is, for the rise, exploits, and doom of Antichrist. They also serve another purpose—to show us how the symbols are to be interpreted. When a prophecy has already been fulfilled, it should not be too difficult to understand.

In Daniel Chapter 2, it was Nebuchadnezzar who saw the vision and Daniel who told the meaning; now in Daniel Chapter 7, it is Daniel who sees the visions and the angel who tells the meaning. The four great beasts are interpreted for us in Daniel 7:17 as four kings which shall rise out of the earth: "These great beasts, which are four, are four kings which shall arise out of the earth." "King" is Daniel's word for empire. As gold is the chief among metals, so the lion is the king of beasts. Both the head of gold and the lion refer to the empire of Nebuchadnezzar, Babylon.

And had eagle's wings refers possibly to the speed with which Nebuchadnezzar acquired his kingdom. The wings apply to the king himself, who was a great man of many talents, and who was king of one of the greatest cities ever built. Daniel's word-pictures are very much like present-day cartoons, except that they are in words instead of drawings. As the lion marked *Babylon*, so eagle's wings marked the *greatness* of Nebuchadnezzar.

I beheld till the wings thereof were plucked. This is best understood from the actual record of Nebuchadnezzar. We have definite information about Nebuchadnezzar so that the phrase, "his wings were plucked," is best understood from that record, made by the king in connection with his proclamation concerning the greatness of God:

> The king spake, and said, Is not this great Babylon, that I have built for the house of the kingdom by the might of my power, and for the honour of my majesty? While the word was in the king's mouth, there fell a voice from heaven, saying, O king Nebuchadnezzar, to thee it is spoken; The kingdom is departed from thee.
>
> And they shall drive thee from men, and thy dwelling shall be with the beasts of the field: they shall make thee to eat grass as oxen, and seven times shall pass over thee, until thou know that the most High ruleth in the kingdom of men, and giveth it to whomsoever he will.
>
> The same hour was the thing fulfilled upon Nebuchadnezzar: and he was driven from men, and did eat grass as oxen, and his body was wet with the dew of heaven, till his hairs were grown like eagles' feathers, and his nails like birds' claws. —Dan. 4:30–33.

And it was lifted up from the earth, and made to stand upon the feet as a man, and a man's heart was given to it. Again, this passage is best explained in the words of King Nebuchadnezzar himself:

> At the end of the days I Nebuchadnezzar lifted up mine eyes unto heaven, and *mine understanding returned unto me,* and I blessed the most High and I praised and honoured him that liveth for ever, . . .
>
> *At the same time my reason returned unto me;* and for the glory of my kingdom, mine honour and brightness returned unto me; and my counsellors and my lords sought unto me; and I was established in my kingdom, and excellent majesty was added unto me.
>
> Now I Nebuchadnezzar praise and extol and honour the King of heaven, all whose works are truth, and his ways judgment: and those that walk in pride he is able to abase. —Dan. 4:34–37.

THE SECOND BEAST—A BEAR

And behold another beast, a second, like unto a bear, and it raised up itself on one side, and it had three ribs in the mouth of it between the teeth of it: and they said thus unto it, Arise, devour much flesh. —Dan. 7:5.

The second beast, a bear, corresponds to the silver of the image of Daniel Chapter 2, and is a symbol of the empire of Cyrus the Persian and Darius the Mede. This was known as the Persian Empire, or the empire of the Medes and Persians.

And it raised up itself on one side, or, "it raised up one dominion"—that is, one out of two. There were two sides; the bear got up, first on one side, then on the other. If this were a cartoon, the two sides would be labeled Media and Persia. Media was the older country; it came up first. Persia followed, and the two became one empire. This is the same idea that was symbolized by the two arms of the image uniting in the breast, except that the arms could not show the movement or how the empire was formed. It is important to note this, because future and more difficult revelations will follow the same process. We are always passing from the known to the unknown.

And it had three ribs in the mouth of it. These empires did not cover the same territory, for empires were always extending themselves. These ribs show the *new* territory taken over by the new empire. The movement was generally toward the west, as you will note on the maps. The ribs might be labeled Babylon, Lydia, and Egypt.

THE THIRD BEAST—A LEOPARD

After this I beheld, and lo another, like a leopard, which had upon the back of it four wings of a fowl; the beast had also four heads; and dominion was given to it. —Dan. 7:6.

This leopard corresponds to the brass of the image of Daniel Chapter 2. It represents the empire of Alexander, the Grecian Empire.

The beast had also four heads; and dominion was given to it. After the death of Alexander, the empire divided into four parts represented here by the four heads of the beast.

THE FOURTH BEAST—DREADFUL AND TERRIBLE

After this I saw in the night visions, and behold a fourth beast, dreadful and terrible, and strong exceedingly; and it had great iron teeth: it devoured and brake in pieces, and stamped the residue with the feet of it: and it was diverse from all the beasts that were before it; and it had ten horns.
—Dan. 7:7.

The fourth beast is not named but is called simply a beast. It corresponds to the image's legs of iron and represents the fourth world-empire (the Roman). Iron is again mentioned as characteristic of this empire.

It had great iron teeth. Rome ruled with an iron hand. The book of Acts reveals with what fear and respect the Roman Caesar was held by those even as far away as Palestine and Syria.

It devoured and brake in pieces and stamped the residue with the feet of it. A good illustration of this is found in the siege and destruction of Jerusalem in 70 A.D., and in the scattering of the Jews, upon whom the feet of the beast are still stamping.

The Roman Empire was different from the other empires in many respects. It bore somewhat the nature of a republic. (There was a senate, and there was the possibility of being a citizen rather than a subject.) It was not the creation of one man as were the others; it had no successor and will have no successor until it succeeds itself.

It was diverse from all the beasts that were before it. There is a strikingly similar statement to this in H. G. Wells' *Outline of History*. Mr. Wells writes, "Now this new Roman power which arose to dominate the western world was in several respects *a different thing* from any of the great empires that had hitherto prevailed in the civilized world."

Ten Horns

And it had ten horns. The meaning of the horns is the same as that of the ten toes of the image of Daniel Chapter 2. A horn refers to power. The beast represents the empire; its horns represent the separate countries that make up the empire.

It is unnecessary to count the countries of Europe, Africa, and the Middle East and try to make them number exactly ten, for the number is continually changing and does not have to be exactly ten at any particular time. In prophecy, *ten* is usually a round number, not indicating a definite amount. "Ye shall have tribulation *ten* days" (Rev. 2:10). When we are told that the Lord will come with *ten* thousand of His saints, we do not suppose that some saints will be left behind, or that the total number of saints is only ten thousand. It indicates a large but indefinite number. Ten is used in the same way in the parable of the ten virgins.

The ten *toes* represent all the countries into which the Roman Empire divided. The ten *horns* represent the same countries. It is possible that in the end they will number exactly ten.

So far in Daniel's second vision (ch. 7), little new material has been added that was not covered by the image of Chapter 2. Every feature is parallel to the image. It should be noted, however, that the ten horns coming out of the head of the beast do *not* represent the revival of the empire, for the ten horns have been in existence ever since the Roman

Empire fell apart. The ten *horns* correspond to the ten *toes,* and the ten toes represent the *dividing* of the kingdom.

This much of the prophecy has been fulfilled, but from verse 8 on to the end of the chapter, everything concerning the vision and its interpretation is new material not mentioned hitherto. What follows verse 7 is future. That which Daniel saw was not the immediate revival of the empire but the arrival of a man. From now on, all the attention is centered around this one man. If there is any revival of the Roman Empire, it will be his work. *It is not the empire that produces the man, but the man who constructs an empire.*

This man is the most sensational figure in prophecy. He figures in the prophecies concerning the Jews, concerning the nations, and concerning the Church. To trace his character and his actions would take us into many parts of the Bible. Some things said about him are so unbelievable that they have seldom been taken at face value. His rise will probably be the most spectacular and world-shaking spectacle that has ever happened. It is only since the invention of the H-bomb that we have been able to see how some of the prophecies could possibly be true. All the world will wonder at him, "whose coming is after the working of Satan" (II Thess. 2:9).

Another Little Horn—Antichrist

I considered the horns, and, behold, there came up among them another little horn, before whom there were three of the first horns plucked up by the roots: and, behold, in this horn were eyes like the eyes of a man, and a mouth speaking great things. —Dan. 7:8.

I considered the horns. Daniel had no map of Europe nor any conception of how Europe would look in 2500 years. There were no newspapers, no radios, and no weekly magazines to keep him posted. If Daniel had had a map, he would not have needed the symbol.

There is only limited value in trying to draw a picture of a hideous beast with horns coming out of his head. As a matter of fact, we have something better than the picture of a symbol—a picture of the fulfillment. What we want to know, after all, is the fulfillment—what the symbol means. Daniel "considered" the horns. We follow Daniel's example when we consider and study a map of what the horns stood for.

Daniel was not interested in any movement among the horns that left them intact—as all wars to date have done. War after war has raged across Europe, but after each was over, the nations were still there. A few border lines may have been changed, but the nations were still intact. These wars were unimportant as far as this prophecy is concerned; they were not noted by Daniel.

Antichrist's Origin

And, behold, there came up among them another little horn. This is the beginning of the end. Here is the man who completely represents Satan. From now on, all earthly events revolve around him; he will continue to grow in power and arrogance till Christ comes. His destruction is the climax of Daniel's prophecies: "I beheld, and the same horn made war with the saints, and *prevailed against them; until the Ancient of days came,* and judgment was given to the saints of the most High; and the time came that the saints possessed the kingdom" (Dan. 7:21, 22).

It should be noted that the symbol, "little horn," applies equally well to the nation and to the man. (This is true in both Daniel and Revelation.) In a dictatorship, it is not necessary to distinguish between the dictator and the nation. We often speak of the man at the head of a nation when our words imply that we are thinking of what the nation is doing. Daniel used the symbols of gold and silver in the same way. He said to Nebuchadnezzar, "*Thou* art this head of gold, and after thee shall arise *another kingdom* [Medo-Persia] inferior to thee." The man and the kingdom answer to the same symbol. (This is true throughout the Bible. The meaning can be ascertained from the context.) In the Scriptures we sometimes encounter the neuter gender first: "it" had ten horns; then, at a certain point, a change is made to the masculine gender: I beheld even till the beast was slain and "his" body destroyed (vs. 11). The *man* soon becomes more important than the *nation* or all the nations.

The man must have a country. He is, after all, a dictator over one nation. Primarily, the horns are nations. "Another" horn would be another nation. But soon the "man" emerges as the dominant factor, and from then on, it is the man, not the nation, that is seen by the prophet.

"Another" horn would be an eleventh, yet never are there said to be eleven horns. The man becomes the beast itself, and is called the beast in Revelation. This man becomes personally so powerful that he *is* the empire out of which come the ten horns. So we start with a nation; we end with a man. This man is revealed in Revelation to be somewhat more than a man, even more than a satanic man. He becomes the embodiment of Satan himself.

"There came up *among /between/ them*, another little horn" (Dan. 7:8). This new nation is not one of the ten, but is close to them—so close, in fact, that it borders upon them and possibly juts down into their midst. We must look for this country on the very edge of (if not partially in) the Roman Empire. If it were actually a part of the Roman Empire, it would be counted as one of the ten horns and so could not be "another" one. On the other hand, if it were totally outside the Roman Empire, it could not be said to come "out of" the head of the beast. So to say that the little horn is *another* horn (coming up "between" the others, which come out of the head of the beast) is just another way of saying that this new country is both inside and outside the Roman Empire.

An illustration—not necessarily a fulfillment—of this peculiarity is Germany, a portion of which was in the Roman Empire, and thus actually "between" the horns. Germany comes "out of" the head of the beast, yet could be another horn.

(Please note: I cite this only as an illustration. The actual fulfillment is not in sight at this writing—although there are many considerations that point in the same direction. The place of the rise of Antichrist is indicated with enough precision, if you put all the prophecies together, so that you will be able to recognize the place when it happens.)

Another little horn. This new horn is small at the start but soon becomes *"more stout than his fellows"* (vs. 20). We might say it is small but strong, and, most important of all, has a will to conquer.

Bible prophecy is rich in detail at this point, but much of it is lost to students because of interpretations which, at best, can satisfy only a portion of the prophecy. It has become necessary to adopt a very strict rule and apply it to all Old Testament prophecy. This is the rule of interpretation: *If a prophecy has not been completely fulfilled in the past, then it is to be fulfilled in the future.* If this is not true, then a large section of prophecy is unreliable. A partially fulfilled prophecy is unreliable. A partially fulfilled prophecy is not a fulfilled prophecy. No prophecy is fulfilled at all until it is fulfilled completely. (It should be noted, however, that Jesus' coming to earth is in two parts (His first coming, and His second coming); sometimes a portion of a prophecy is fulfilled at each coming.)

It is true that a similar set of circumstances may have been fulfilled in the past, and we may think of them as a partial fulfillment. They may be used for purposes of illustration, but they should not be allowed to confuse the real

	Chapter 2	Chapter 7	Chapter 8
1st Empire Babylonian	Head of Gold Dan. 2:31, 32, 37, 38	LION Dan. 7:1–4	
2nd Empire Medo-Persian	Arms of Silver Dan. 2:32, 39	BEAR Two Sides Dan. 7:5	RAM Two Horns Dan. 8:3, 20
3rd Empire Grecian	Trunk of Brass Dan. 2:32, 39	LEOPARD Four Heads Dan. 7:6	GOAT Four Horns Dan. 8:5, 8, 21
4th Empire Roman	Legs of Iron Dan. 2:33, 40	BEAST Dan. 7:7	
Divided Empire	Ten Toes Iron and Clay Dan. 2:33, 41	TEN HORNS Dan. 7:7	In the latter time of their kingdom; when the transgressor are come to the full Dan. 8:23
Rise of Antichrist		LITTLE HORN Out of the head of the beast Mouth speaking great things Subdue three kings Dan. 7:8	LITTLE HORN Out of one of the four w Waxes great Destroy wonderful thing * * * Peace and Craft Dan. 8:9, 18–25
Rapture Revelation of the Man of sin		THRONES CAST DOWN Judgment Throne set up Action starts in Heaven Books opened Dan. 7:9–14	STARS CAST DO Dan. 8:10–12
Tribulation Day of the Lord		TRIBULATION SAINTS Dan. 7:24, 25	DESTROY HOLY PEOPLE Abomination of Desolat Dan. 8:12–14, 24
Kingdom of Christ and The Saints	Stone Cut Out Without Hand Becomes Mountain Dan. 2:34, 35, 44, 45	JUDGMENT OF BEAST Saints possess the Kingdom Dan. 7:26, 27	ANTICHRIST DESTROYED Without Hand Dan. 8:25

Chapter 11	Revelation	Olivet Discourse — Others
	Mouth as the mouth of a lion Rev. 13:2	
INGS OF PERSIA Dan. 11:2	Feet as the feet of a bear Rev. 13:2	
MIGHTY KING Dan. 11:3, 4	Like unto a leopard Rev. 13:2	
TERVENING WARS NG OF THE NORTH Dan. 11:15–19	Beast out of the sea Rev. 13:1	
all of the Roman Empire Dan. 11:19	Seven heads and ten horns Crowns on his horns Rev. 13:1	
AISER OF TAXES the glory of the kingdom Dan. 11:20	Dragon gave him his throne Rev. 13:2 Mouth speaking great things Rev. 13:5	Wars and Commotions Matt. 24:6; Luke 21:9 Peace and Safety I Thess. 5:3
Antichrist killed: neither in anger nor in battle Dan. 11:20 ATAN REVEALED A Vile Person Dan. 11:21, 22	Man child caught up to heaven War in heaven Satan cast down to the earth Rev. 12:5, 7–10 Head wounded and healed Rev. 13:3	As in the days of Noah One taken, another left Matt. 24:37–41 Escape from a time of trouble Dan. 12:1; Isa. 26:19–21 Zeph. 2:3
RS OF ANTICHRIST Dan. 11:23–43	Opens his mouth in blasphemy against God Makes war with the saints Rev. 13:6, 7	Tribulation Saints killed Nation against nation Kingdom against kingdom Time of trouble such as never was Matt. 24:7–10, 21
Armies gathered against Jerusalem ANTICHRIST MES TO HIS END Dan. 11:44, 45	Antichrist cast into the lake of fire Rev. 19:20	Armies against Jerusalem Luke 21:20 Ezek. 38:8, 9; Zech. 14:2 Coming of Christ with the Saints Matt. 24:29–31

issue. Too many times these similar incidents have been treated as final fulfillments. This is done by taking them out of their context and treating them merely as separate verses, a practice carried on by many who should know better. Actually, instead of supporting the Bible, it puts a cloud over some very important passages and makes even some simple prophecies difficult to explain.

There came up . . . another little horn, before whom there were three of the first horns plucked up by the roots. Verse 24 says of the little horn, "He shall be diverse from the first, and he shall subdue three kings." The fourth beast was diverse from the first three. This difference was mainly in the kind of government. Each of the first three world-empires was largely the work of *one* man—Nebuchadnezzar, Cyrus, Alexander; however, the Roman Empire was *not* the domain or work of one man. Although it was more powerful than any of the others, it was more like a republic than a kingdom.

Yet in the case of the little horn, the situation is again reversed. The little horn is an absolute dictator, while the other horns may be more or less democratic. The little horn represents a move back to strong, one-man government when *one man* will dominate *the world.*

For more than a generation now, the world has been moving slowly but surely toward that end. The rise of dictators one after another is not an accident. It is a trend, a general movement toward a definite goal. Satan is probing.

Churches are also moving in the direction of world organization—one church—with great power in the hands of a few. In America, which is the very bulwark of democracy, the trend is away from state sovereignty toward a strong central government. It seems to be irresistible. No matter how strong the pronouncements are which a candidate may make before election, he always slides into the groove, and before long is advocating, even insisting upon, more power for Washington at the expense of the states. All this is background for Antichrist. It indicates a trend.

And he shall subdue three kings (nations). In the vision, "another little horn" pulled up three horns by the roots. If we applied arithmetic at this point, we would get *ten* plus *one* equals *eleven*, minus *three* equals *eight*. Therefore it would seem that eight nations will be left. But it does not work that way. Ten is a round number, so that the actual number is not important. (It is only important that we know who are represented by the horns. Of course, in the end, the number may be exactly ten (Rev. 17:16).*

Antichrist's empire will theoretically include all the territory covered by *all* four prophetic empires, although he will always have trouble holding it together. There will be wars.

When Revelation tells the story of the rise of the final kingdom, it describes it by naming again all the beasts of Daniel. Revelation 13 is strikingly like Daniel 7:2, 3. The differences are due to the point of time. John was looking *backwards* over all time; Daniel was looking *forward* from his time. The added feature in Revelation is the seven heads— seven indicating completeness. "I stood upon the sand of the sea, and saw a beast rise up out of the sea, *having seven heads and ten horns,* and upon his horns ten crowns, and upon his heads the name of blasphemy" (Rev. 13:1). Revelation is a book of consummations. There the whole subject is in view. Seven is the number of completeness or perfection in the sense of totality. Before the time of Daniel, there were two world-empires (Assyria and Egypt); Daniel lived in the time of the two empires (Babylon and Persia) and saw two (Greece and Rome) prophetically. Before Christ comes there will be one more world-empire.

---

*And the ten horns which thou sawest upon the beast, these shall hate the whore, and shall make her desolate and naked, and shall eat her flesh, and burn her with fire. —Rev. 17:16.

This "seventh head" of Revelation is Daniel's beast that has ten horns. But there it is seen in its final form, *after* the little horn has taken over. This is sometimes referred to as the revival of the Roman Empire. While Daniel sees the whole history of this fourth beast, Revelation deals with it only at "the time of the end" when Antichrist rebuilds the empire. It is then that "the *beast* which I saw was like unto a *leopard,* and his feet were as the feet of a *bear.* and his mouth as the mouth of a *lion;* and the dragon gave him his power, and his seat [throne], and great authority" (Rev. 13:2). The beast, the leopard, the bear, and the lion—these are the four world-empires of Babylon, Persia, Greece, and Rome. This is a revival not only of the Roman Empire but of all the world-empires under one head. This corresponds to Daniel 2:45.* When the stone strikes, the whole image is standing again.

The little horn becoming the beast may seem a little ambiguous, but it is exactly what happens. At this point it would be well to study the symbolism, comparing Daniel and Revelation. We are dealing with a rather complicated series of events. Only symbols would be adequate to express it so far in advance.

There is first the beast of Daniel 7, the fourth world-empire. Out of that empire come ten nations (or more)—ten horns. So far we are dealing with past history. Then (and this is future) there will come up another horn (or nation), small but strong. This is "the little horn." It will be dominated by one man who will be so powerful that no one can stand against him. He will weld together an empire bigger than the ten horns, but he still will have the ten horns. He will become a beast with ten horns. It is just at this point that he appears in Revelation.

---

*Forasmuch as thou sawest that the stone was cut out of the mountain without hands, and that it brake in pieces the iron, the brass, the clay, the silver, and the gold; the great God hath made known to the king what shall come to pass hereafter: and the dream is certain, and the interpretation thereof sure. —Dan. 2:45.

(There are other complications which eventually we must consider, because we are dealing with Satan as well as with man. The more powerful and effective our modern weapons become, the more amazing will be this man's military marvels—they are "out of this world." But for now, our inquiry must run along another line.)

Behold, in this horn were eyes like the eyes of a man. The first beast, the lion, was given a *man's* heart. This little horn has a *man's* eyes. The "man's heart" evidently refers to the excellent character of the king, demonstrated in his public confession of God. Though this little horn retains his beastly heart, yet he has the eyes of a man. The eyes are a part of the symbol. (We would expect a man to have eyes.) Usually, eyes refer to intelligence, and that would probably be the meaning of eyes in a symbol. This feature is explained in the next vision: He will understand dark sentences (Dan. 8:23).*

This is satanic intelligence. His coming is "after the working of Satan" and his power will be due to his super knowledge. This is no ordinary individual. Man's knowledge is reaching tremendous heights and depths. Today this knowledge is being directed toward implements of destruction. So great has been the progress (?) that no one in the world is safe. Man, and hence Satan, can now actually wipe life off the face of the earth. If this is *not* the end of the age, how can we go beyond it? We have reached the ultimate.

The world is coming right up to the brink of disaster. It is Satan's big chance. He will rule the world if he can, destroy it if he must. Antichrist will "save" the world. He is *"the"* man of his day. He will know something beyond what the scientists have done. He is able to make war successfully, suddenly, dramatically, almost singlehandedly, against the best that science can produce. Scientists will

*And in the latter time of their kingdom, when the transgressors are come to the full, a king of fierce countenance, and understanding dark sentences, shall stand up. —Dan. 8:23.

produce the ultimate weapon and Antichrist will go them one better. "And they worshipped the beast saying, . . .who is able to make war with him?" (Rev. 13:4); "Their [his] horsemen shall come from far: they shall fly" (Hab. 1:8).

Again let me illustrate. (Please bear in mind that this is an illustration; it is not given as a fulfillment.) Pierre Van Paassen, author of *The Forgotten Ally,* wrote: "I had just talked with Adolph Hitler in Bonn after one of his propaganda meetings. He upbraided me violently for daring to defend the Jews in his presence. 'You, who are an Aryan, a Nordic, a Teuton from the shores of the German Ocean!' he screamed, 'why do you not see the menace of the Jew to our western civilization?' In his eyes I had seen the strange, unearthly fire of hatred and was convinced that the man would before long be the master of Germany. . . . Not a Jew will be seen in the Reich in ten years. Even Jewish names on the tombstones will be obliterated. . . . I say so because I have looked in the eyes of Adolph Hitler."

Although the eyes are a part of the symbol and therefore do not necessarily refer to the eyes of the man himself, eyes do reflect the inner man. His diabolical intelligence would be reflected in the eyes, and so one of the outstanding features of this man when he appears may be his eyes. This is the more likely because of the next characteristic of the little horn.

And a mouth speaking great things. He literally talks his way into power by flatteries, promises of peace and prosperity. Daniel develops this in his next vision (chapter 8). This feature of the little horn is also a feature of the man. "I beheld then because of the voice of *the great words* which the horn spake" (Dan. 7:11). "And there was given unto him a mouth speaking great things . . . and he opened his mouth in blasphemy against God" (Rev. 13:5, 6).

These two special features of the horn, "a mouth speaking great things," and "eyes like the eyes of a man," are also the outstanding features of the man. When he comes, you will probably hear a lot of talk about his eyes, and he will "do things" to people. These two features are the identifying marks by which you may know him, although there will be no mistaking him because the prophecies are so specific. This man is a "natural." He perfectly fits the times. He is just what the nations want—a man who can free the world from fear—terrible fear of impending destruction—and bring to the nations wealth—amazing wealth. The world has never seen or dreamed of the kind of wealth this man will be able to produce. They will even trim their buildings with gold.

The potential is being built up now. It is forming in so many places with such fantastic new discoveries and inventions that we simply cannot keep up with them. The General Electric Company says that it is going to produce more in the next ten years than in all the previous seventy-five years of its existence. This is largely because of the marvelous new things it sees on the horizon. Atomic batteries, which never need recharging, will furnish power in all places, however remote.

All that the world needs today is a man capable of enforcing peace, along with a free transfer of goods to the world's markets. Then in a few years this world could be transformed into a paradise, every square mile of it. This peace and security will be Satan's great false millennium by which he will deceive the whole world. Paul says, "When they shall say, Peace and safety; *then sudden destruction cometh upon them*" (I Thess. 5:3). This is such an important subject of prophecy that a whole chapter of Revelation is given over entirely to it (chapter 18). With such a program as this to offer the world, it will not be necessary for the little horn to do much conquering by military force. "Through *his policy* also he shall cause craft to prosper in his hand" (Dan. 8:25).

How can such a vast empire be acquired by pulling up by the roots only three horns? The fact is that this man will not actually acquire the empire by conquest but rather by what comes out of his mouth. It is evident that most of the countries involved will be almost automatically on the side of the little horn, as a result of a powerful common enemy that had been on the point of destroying them. But there may be some captive countries that would not have a free choice until they were conquered. It would be necessary to pull up these horns by the roots. At the time of the rise of Antichrist there will be three countries that for some reason cannot be classed with the others. These may be countries of the Roman Empire occupied by some foreign power.

The reason these three countries have to be conquered may be the key to the whole prophetic setup. Why should they be so different from the others? Even now as this is being written, all of the land we are talking about—all the lands of prophecy—are beginning to band together in various groups for mutual protection against Russia. The conspicuous exceptions are those now occupied by Russia. They are three in number: Hungary, Rumania, and Bulgaria. (There are others, but they were not in the Roman Empire.) Before the final events start to happen, we do not know what changes will take place; but before that day, many changes might come.

The Scene Changes to Heaven

I beheld till the thrones were cast down, and the Ancient of days did sit, whose garment was white as snow, and the hair of his head like the pure wool: his throne was like the fiery flame, and his wheels as burning fire. A fiery stream issued and came forth from before him: thousand thousands ministered unto him, and ten thousand times ten thousand stood before him: the judgment was set, and the books were opened. —Dan. 7:9–10.

The scene now changes suddenly. Daniel breaks into the story about the little horn to record a scene in heaven

(Dan. 7:9, 10). The fact that the narrative is interrupted shows that the events in heaven are to take place at the same time as the events on earth. While the little horn is establishing himself on earth, preparations are being made in heaven to dislodge him.

Skip the two verses on the scene in heaven, and the story narrative is continuous. Verse 8 says, "In this horn [was] *a mouth speaking great things.*" Verse 11 says, "I beheld then because of *the voice of the great words* which the horn spake."

The break in the story here is to tell of something else happening in heaven at the same time.

In vision, Daniel first saw the little horn beginning to consolidate his new empire by his eyes and by his mouth. Then Daniel looked up and was given a vision of what would be happening in heaven at the same time. In heaven will be great activity. (What Daniel saw is described by John more fully in Revelation, Chapters 4 and 5. John saw the same scene and set it forth in greater detail.) The time of this heavenly scene is immediately after the resurrection of the dead and the catching up of the living saints. The Resurrection is not actually in view here because the Church is not involved with this prophecy; the tribulation saints are mentioned later. In the scene in verse 9 we are approaching the "day of the Lord." Satan is not to go unchallenged; God will have His answer for the great words which the little horn will speak.

I beheld till thrones were cast down. "Cast down" could mean "set *down*," or it could mean "put in place," that is, "set *up*." This is exactly what will happen after the Resurrection. The judgment throne of God will be set up, encircled by twenty-four other thrones (erroneously translated "seats" in the A.V.). From these thrones, judgment will proceed.

But thrones will be cast down, for the principalities and powers of Satan in heavenly places will be cast down to the earth (Rev. 12:7–11).* Thrones, therefore, will be set up, and thrones will also be cast down. At the present time Satan is the prince of the power of the air. His principalities are in the heavens, and he rules over a vast domain. Revelation seems to teach that his fall will carry with him one-third of the angels. This would be a tremendous number, running into astronomical figures, and would probably cover a large territory.

The Resurrection will produce a crisis in Satan's realm—an all-out war, in fact.

> There was war in heaven: Michael and his angels fought against the dragon; and the dragon fought and his angels, and prevailed not; neither was their place found any more in heaven. And *the great dragon was cast out,* that old serpent, called the Devil, and Satan, which deceiveth the whole world: *he was cast out into the earth, and his angels were cast out with him....* Therefore rejoice, ye heavens, and ye that dwell in them. Woe to the inhabiters of the earth and of the sea! for the devil is come down unto you, having great wrath, because he knoweth that he hath but a short time.
> —Rev. 12:7–9, 12.

And the Ancient of days did sit. The description of the throne in Daniel is similar to that of Revelation but differs in some details. This difference is to be expected, because no words are adequate to the task of picturing such a scene. Whenever *heavenly* scenes are described, they have to be put into *earthly* words; but actually there are no such words,

---

*And there was war in heaven: Michael and his angels fought against the dragon; and the dragon fought and his angels, and prevailed not; neither was their place found anymore in heaven. And the great dragon was cast out, that old serpent, called the Devil, and Satan, which deceiveth the whole world. he was cast out into the earth, and his angels were cast out with him. And I heard a loud voice saying in heaven, Now is come salvation and strength, and the kingdom of our God, and the power of his Christ: for the accuser of our brethren is cast down, which accused them before our God day and night. And they overcame him by the blood of the Lamb, and by the word of their testimony; and they loved not their lives unto the death. —Rev. 12:7–11. (See **All Things New,** Rev. 12 and 13.)

and so a writer would have to use something out of his own experience. Two viewers, therefore, would not describe the same scene in exactly the same words, for each would pick words from his own vocabulary. In both Daniel 7 and Revelation 12, the time and the place are the same, as well as the events that follow. John and Daniel saw the same thing.

Whose garment was white as snow and the hair of his head like pure wool. This is not the "great white throne," though in each case white seems to be a dominant factor. *White* connects with righteousness but also connects with judgment; in fact, righteousness and judgment are akin. Judgment proceeds from the righteousness of God.

A *white* robe will be the garment of the Judge; it will also be the garment of the saints who have put on the righteousness of Christ. A white robe of righteousness will admit the saints into the marriage supper of the Lamb. The white garment worn by the Judge will condemn Satan, Antichrist, and his followers.

His throne was like a fiery flame, and his wheels as burning fire. A fiery stream issued and came forth from before him. The One who will sit on the throne will hold the book with seven seals. Daniel's account is greatly condensed; Revelation expands the scene into the seven last plagues (trumpets and vials), all of which will be connected with fire. In the redemption of the earth, fire will be the purging element.

Thousand thousands ministered unto him and ten thousand times ten thousand stood before him. This is identical with Revelation: "I beheld and I heard the voice of many angels round about the throne and the beasts and the elders: and the number of them was ten thousand times ten thousand, and thousands of thousands" (Rev. 5:11).

The judgment was set and the books were opened. The seals will be broken. Revelation mentions only one book at this point; other books come later. Of course Daniel is putting it all into one short sentence: "The judgment was set." Judgment will actually start with the house of God. The Resurrection will be a judgment because some will be taken and some will be left. In the parable in Matthew 25, the ten virgins were all in one group until the announcement of the bridegroom caused a separation.

At that same time, the servant who says, "My Lord delayeth his coming," will meet his judgment. He is *among* the saved, but he is not *one* of the saved. He will be left behind and appointed his place among the hypocrites. This will be his judgment—even though its execution will await his death.

Many among the dead will be in the same classification as the five foolish virgins and the evil servant. In the parables, these are symbolized as bad fish, or tares, or a man without a wedding garment, or an unprofitable servant, etc. At the time of the Resurrection, they will also be separated— in this case separated by the angels (not by themselves). The dead are separated by force; the living separate themselves. The living are not condemned to the furnace of fire or to outer darkness, for that kind of judgment comes only after death.

If there are tares among the wheat, they will be separated, whether they be living or dead. But if they are living, they will separate themselves and be left behind; and if they are dead, they will be gathered out by the angels before the "saints go marching in."

> As therefore the tares are gathered and burned in the fire; so shall it be in the end of this world [age]. The Son of man shall send forth his angels, and they shall gather out of his kingdom all things that offend, and them which do iniquity; and shall cast them into a furnace of fire: there shall be wailing and gnashing of teeth. Then shall the righteous shine forth as the sun in the kingdom of their Father. —Matt. 13: 40–43.

It was this separation that the angel referred to in Daniel 12: 2: "Many of them that sleep in the dust of the earth shall awake, *some* to everlasting life, and *some* to shame and everlasting contempt."

After this judgment within the house of God, the judgment of the living nations will begin. This will take some time and will pass through a number of phases. One of these phases will be cleansing the earth from the results of sin. In this judgment Satan, fallen angels, and demons will also be involved. Again, let us repeat that Revelation goes into great detail; Daniel saw only a glimpse of the whole scene—that which applied to the little horn and his kingdom.

Great Words and Deeds of the Horn

I beheld then because of the voice of the great words which the horn spake: I beheld even till the beast was slain, and his body destroyed and given to the burning flame.
—Dan. 7:11.

The voice of the great words which the horn spake. After the scene in heaven, verses 9 and 10, the story on earth is continued. In the next verse Daniel covers all the time from the rise of the little horn on earth to his final disposition at the time of the return of Christ. Many of the acts of the little horn are told by Daniel later. (Revelation completes the story.) The point that Daniel stresses here is the matter of "the great words." What these words will be is only now becoming apparent.

The little horn must be identified with Satan. In Revelation the little horn is part of the satanic trinity. By a process of death and resurrection, Satan will actually take over a man's body, so that the little horn will become Satan incarnate—whom we call Antichrist.

The one thing said about Satan when he is cast out of heaven is that he will deceive the whole world (Rev. 12:9). This deceit of the last days is mentioned often by the prophets, and especially by Jesus and by Paul. His deceit will be propagated by words—great deceiving by "great" words. We have mild examples of this kind of great words in party platforms and campaign speeches. An even better example would be the speeches of Hitler.

The little horn will be a spellbinder. But his promises will also have substance, for he will be able to "make them good." His power will be supernatural because "his coming will be after the working of Satan" (II Thess. 2:9). He will be able to command help from sources unknown in the world since the tower of Babel.

It is impossible to exaggerate this point. We are dealing now with the fact that the greatest forces of evil will be in possession of the earth, and will be locked in mortal combat with the greatest forces of heaven. By shifting the scene from earth to heaven and then back to earth again, Daniel brings these powers together.

What we today think of as miraculous will be commonplace in those days. Spirits have great power over material things, and even now this power is being demonstrated in the heavens. At that time, Satan will make an image live and talk, so that "they that dwell on the earth shall wonder" after the beast. ("Beast" is the Revelation name for "the little horn.")

Antichrist's Promises of World Prosperity

Probably Satan's most effective "great words" will be promises of peace and prosperity—a false millennium. Even now, *that* is the only issue that gets votes. It will be still more effective if the world faces seeming certain destruction.

As an example, imagine what would happen if the cold war should come to an end by military moves on the part of Russia, who is bent on conquering the world. She could start little wars in so many places at once that we would be in a state of utter confusion. Added to this would be the terror of not knowing what would happen next. At the same time, the 25,000 trained or instructed Communists in this country would go into action with a prepared plan that would paralyze every industry, blow up every bridge, and contaminate the water supply of cities. The 300,000 ex-Communists would suddenly drop the *ex*. The same thing would happen in nearly every country of the world. (This might not all happen here, but the threat of it would be terrifying.) There would be a depression such as this world has never experienced. The threat of imminent and sudden horrible destruction by H-bombs or germ warfare would be enough to paralyze the country so that the wheels of industry could not turn, and people would be on the verge of starvation.

Today America seems to be prosperous, but millions of people depend for their very existence on the smooth working of our transportation system. Cities do not have food for more than a few days.

We are struggling with problems of over-production of foodstuffs and of trying to get farmers to curtail production— even paying them for it. At the same time, we do not have enough food stored in homes (where it can be readily obtained) to last a month. Most homes have none. We have no "Joseph" in Washington. If we are going to be taxed to pay farmers for raising or not raising food, then the people who pay for that food by taxes should have it stored in their basements or in community storehouses, where transportation will not be a factor.

The sudden rise of a man who could handle a world situation of that kind, and who could restore peace and safety by a superhuman power, would captivate the imagination of the world. *"Who is like unto the beast?"*

Preparations for war bring out new things and develop the world's resources faster than peaceful progress. Two world wars and the cold war have completely changed the whole world. Before World War I, about two-thirds of the population of the world was asleep. It had no interest in world affairs and wanted merely to be left alone. The thought of bettering itself had not occurred to it.

This has all changed. Now all people everywhere are demanding a share of the world's wealth and potential prosperity, and all nations are awake to world movements and the possibilities of a better life. These nations are all rich in natural resources.

Such a world awakening would naturally bring a prosperity involving tremendous wealth. For instance, it has been estimated that to raise India's standard of living by ten per cent would keep our factories going day and night for ten years. This great surge has been held in check by the attempt of certain countries to dominate the whole. An economy of planned poverty has held back world prosperity.

In the meantime, new discoveries and inventions are about to revolutionize our lives. Cheap power is now becoming available for any part of the world no matter how remote. No people will have to wait for transmission lines to be put up or railroads to be built. All nations can have everything at once.

Potentially, all nations are rich. All that is required is a man who can put down forever the planned poverty theory of communism and enforce a world peace with free trade and total opportunity. What would then happen is almost beyond imagination. From the standpoint of space given to it, this is one of the biggest prophetic subjects in the Bible.

The world will be carried away in a mad rush for wealth. Then we will have cities like the New Babylon (described in Revelation 18 and in Jeremiah 50 and 51), whose buildings will be trimmed with gold—and cities like the New Tyre (Zech. 9:3),* where silver and gold will be as dust in the streets. We will have churches like the Laodiceans, whose

---

*And Tyrus did build herself a strong hold, and heaped up silver as the dust, and fine gold as the mire of the streets. —Zech. 9:3.

members will be rich, and increased with goods, and have need of nothing. Antichrist will produce a world prosperity that will make our conception of the millennium seem like a depression.

No wonder Antichrist is described as having a mouth "speaking great things," and making promises that apparently he will be able to carry out. No wonder, also, that the world will worship Antichrist and treat him as God, so that he is able to sit in the temple of God, showing himself that he is God (II Thess. 2:4).*

The Image Stands Again

As concerning the rest of the beasts, they had their dominion taken away: yet their lives were prolonged for a season and a time. —Dan. 7:12.

The rest of the beasts had their dominion taken away. "The rest of the beasts" would be the lion, the bear, and the leopard—that is, the former world-empires of Babylon, Persia, and Greece. As empires, these have already gone out of existence, but they have remained as separate peoples. In time, these three empires will be restored, but not as they originally were, for their boundaries would overlap. If revived, each would have to be smaller in land area than the ancient empire.

Ancient Babylon still exists under the name of Iraq; Persia is Iran. As for the revival of the old Grecian Empire, the present small country of Greece would probably be counted among the ten horns (though it was only a small part of the Grecian Empire). It would seem that the Grecian Empire may return in the last days to fulfill prophecies concerning a new combination of countries, including Greece, Syria, Egypt, Libya, and Algeria. (These would be under one head.)

---

*Who opposeth and exalteth himself above all that is called God, or that is worshipped; so that he as God sitteth in the temple of God, shewing himself that he is God. —II Thess. 2:4.

For all these lands—Babylon, Persia, and Greece—marvelous comebacks are scheduled. Truly their "lives will be prolonged."

Christ Assumes Control

I saw in the night visions, and, behold, one like the Son of man came with the clouds of heaven, and came to the Ancient of days, and they brought him near before him. And there was given him dominion, and glory, and a kingdom, that all people, nations, and languages, should serve him: his dominion is an everlasting dominion, which shall not pass away, and his kingdom that which shall not be destroyed.
—Dan. 7:13, 14.

I saw in the night visions. There are four parts to this prophecy of Daniel Chapter 7: three separate visions and then the explanation. The *first* vision was of the first three beasts: the lion, bear, and leopard (vs. 2–6). The *second* vision (vs. 7–12), which we just finished discussing, was concerned with the fourth beast, the little horn, and also the scene in heaven. (The vision of the little horn was interrupted to show what was happening in heaven at the same time.) The *third* vision of this chapter (vs. 13 and 14) returns to this heavenly scene. Thus in this chapter we are being treated to a double picture. This is something rare in prophecy (outside of Revelation). On earth something momentous is happening, but in heaven something even more important is happening.

This bringing together of the forces of heaven and earth is very significant. The battle lines are tightly drawn, for this is the battle of the earth. Satan's moves are not only watched; they are matched. His great words are answered. This is the day of action; it is the Day of the Lord.

At the present time, and all through the Dispensation of Grace so far, Satan, from his vantage point in the sky, has conducted a sort of spiritual warfare against a material world.

But everything will change. Satan will be cast out of heaven and *"woe to the inhabiters of the earth, for the devil is come down unto you."*

In the place of Satan's principalities and powers in heavenly places, the throne of God will be set up. Other thrones have been put in place and the judgment is set. There is another difference: The saints, who will now operate from Satan's old vantage ground, will not confine themselves to spiritual warfare. They will use every means at their command, material as well as spiritual—the forces of nature, earthquakes, fire, and falling stars. "But now he hath promised, saying, Yet once more I shake not the earth only, but also heaven" (Heb. 12:26).

This will not just be spiritual against material. Satan is in actual possession of the earth, but Christ is King and the rightful owner. The usurper must be evicted.

These two verses (7:13, 14), then, are a condensation of the entire book of Revelation from Chapter 5 to Chapter 22. In the process of redeeming the earth and preparatory to the work that is to be done (especially against Satan and Antichrist), the throne of God will be set up in a special place near the earth.

Study 5

DANIEL'S SECOND VISION
(Continued)

AN EXPLANATION
Daniel 7:15-28

AN EXPLANATION
Daniel 7:15–28

THE WHOLE MAN

I Daniel was grieved in my spirit in the midst of my body, and the visions of my head troubled me. —Dan. 7:15.

In this verse we see that Daniel recognized spirit and soul and body. The head, or soul, is the seat of knowledge; and when a man comes into contact with the spirit world, he begins to see himself in a truer light. Herein is the evangelistic power of prophecy.

HELP FROM HEAVEN

I came near unto one of them that stood by, and asked him the truth of all this. So he told me, and made me know the interpretation of the things. —Dan. 7:16.

I came near unto one of them that stood by. Daniel does not say that this is a vision. So this may or may not have been a vision. Two *"men"* stood by the disciples when Jesus ascended into heaven and made a statement concerning His coming again (Acts 1:10). These men who stood by Daniel could *not* have been Daniel's companions, for Daniel was the only one to see the visions.

Daniel Chapter 7 is running parallel in all these things to the book of Revelation, for those who stood by John helped him understand too: "One of the seven angels . . . talked with me, saying, Come hither, I will shew thee the bride" (Rev. 21: 9). This *angel* was one of the saints. The word *angel* means "messenger" and is used of others besides created angels. ("Unto the angel of the church of Ephesus write, . . .") When John fell down to worship the angel that showed him these things, the angel said, "See thou do it not; for I am thy fellowservant, and one of thy brethren, the prophets."

If, however, those who stood by Daniel were angels, it was probably Gabriel who did the talking, for it was Gabriel who appeared to Daniel to explain the matter of the 70 weeks (Dan. 9:21). It should possibly be noted here that when Gabriel is mentioned in Daniel 9, he is not called the *angel* Gabriel, but the *man* Gabriel.

Those who stood by Daniel could have been saints, for some were in heaven (Enoch, Moses, and Elijah that we know about). Moses and Elijah stood by Jesus on the Mount of Transfiguration, and two "men" were seen in the tomb after His resurrection. In heaven there are two special witnesses, "anointed ones, that stand by the Lord of the whole earth" (Zech. 4:14).

FOUR KINGS

These great beasts, which are four, are four kings, which shall arise out of the earth. —Dan. 7:17.

These great beasts . . . are four kings. A "king" in Daniel means a kingdom or a succession of kings, as well as the individual ruler or dictator. The exact meaning can be ascertained from the context. These four kings are typical of all kings. No attempt is made to write a history of the world but only to summarize world history by the use of these four types which dominated the world of their day. The time during which these four empires are dormant is passed over rather hurriedly. In a history of the world they may be important, but prophetically Daniel goes into no detail about them. He notices them only as "the days of these kings" until something world-changing happens among them. Then Daniel goes into great detail again. In the "end time," the successors of these four kingdoms will dominate the scene. The great cities of Antichrist will be Babylon and Tyre.

SAINTS POSSESS THE KINGDOM

But the saints of the most High shall take the kingdom, and possess the kingdom for ever, even for ever and ever.
—Dan. 7:18.

The saints of the most High does not refer to the Jewish nation. Israel is an earthly nation; the saints are a royal priesthood. Revelation defines this term *saints* thus: "His *servants* shall *serve* him: and they shall see his face; and his name shall be in their foreheads . . . : and they shall reign for ever and ever" (Rev. 22:3–5).

The saints of the most High will be those who will be with Christ when He comes to reign; they will be the immortals who will have passed through the Resurrection. People living on the earth when Christ comes, whether Jews or Gentiles, will *not* be the saints of the most High, for they will be governed, but the saints will be governors.

The saints . . . shall take the kingdom. The kingdom which the saints possess forever will not be the kingdom of David but the kingdom of God. It will include much more than the limited territory of David and Solomon. It will even take in more than the earth: "I will give him the morning star" (Rev. 2:28).

The "seed plot" of the kingdom will be the earth. For the first thousand years while Satan is chained, this earth will be the scene of action. Not until Satan is finally disposed at the end of the thousand years will the kingdom become eternal and the saints rule from the Holy City. The kingdom of God will be everlasting and ever-expanding, for "of the increase of his government and peace there shall be no end" (Isa. 9:7).

The kingdom of God is greater than man has ever conceived. Of course there are always Bible teachers who want to limit God and who delight to tell us what God can *not* do. The Old Testament, they say, is about the Jews; and God could not mention the Church in the Old Testament, or the saints, or the Resurrection, or anything of that nature. But this is not so. God can talk about anything He wants to at any time He wants to. The New Testament is full of quotations from the Old Testament. Paul supported his "new" doctrine of "justification by faith" by a quotation from Habakkuk: "The just shall live by his faith" (Hab. 2:4). In describing the Resurrection in I Corinthians 15:53, 54,* Paul also quotes Hosea: "I will ransom them from the power of the grave; I will redeem them from death: O death, I will be thy plagues; O grave, I will be thy destruction" (Hos. 13:14).

God does not have three or four distinct and eternally separated plans. It is all one. The kingdom is one; there is *one* plan of redemption; there is *one* Lord; His Name is *one*. The Jews will have a part in the kingdom. Promises made to Abraham and David concern their earthly descendants. The nations will be in the kingdom, and there will be nations and kings on earth forever. Even after the millennium, when the saints have received their eternal rewards and inhabit the Holy City, where they will reign forever, even then we are told, "The nations of them which are saved shall walk in the light of it: and the kings of the earth do bring their glory and honour into it" (Rev. 21:24). There will be saved nations. Jesus said that He would separate the nations as a shepherd divides his sheep from his goats. The nations will go

---

*For this corruptible must put on incorruption, and this mortal must put on immortality. So when this corruptible shall have put on incorruption, and this mortal shall have put on immortality, then shall be brought to pass the saying that is written, Death is swallowed up in victory. —I Cor. 15:53, 54.

on expanding forever. "A little one shall become a thousand, and a small one a strong nation: I the Lord will hasten it in his time" (Isa. 60:22).

The Church will have its part in the Kingdom, the biggest part of all, for the saints will be joint-heirs with Christ. The Kingdom will not be limited to the earth, for there will also be new heavens. All this will be big business, worthy of the Creator of all things, God himself; but it will be one plan, one kingdom, and the saints will be concerned in all of it. The Old Testament is not limited to any one subject or to any one people, for the Bible is one—the product of one mind, and the revelation of one plan.

THE TRUTH OF THE LITTLE HORN

Then I would know the truth of the fourth beast, . . . and of the ten horns . . . , and of the other which came up, and before whom three fell: even of that horn that had eyes, and a mouth that spake very great things, whose look was more stout than his fellows. —Dan. 7:19, 20.

Daniel knew what questions to ask. He wanted to know exactly what we would like to know. In asking the truth of all this, Daniel added some details not previously noted.

The little horn . . . , whose look was more stout than his fellows. The little horn, even though small, has a stout look. In both Daniel and Revelation, the symbol "little horn" may refer either to the man, or to the country, or to both; so the little horn is a man, but also a king or a dictator who will have a country. In fact, he will start with one country—a small but potentially strong one with the will to become big and powerful. His people will be workers, for there will be the atmosphere of aggressiveness, if not of aggression.

Habakkuk suggests that this country will be one that has already been put down: "Lo, I raise up the Chaldeans"

(Hab. 1:6). Chaldean is Habakkuk's name for the little horn, for each prophet who mentions Antichrist has his own name for him. Habakkuk also says of Antichrist, "He is a proud man, neither keepeth at home [tries to spread out and conquer other lands], who enlargeth his desire as hell, and is as death, and cannot be satisfied, but gathereth unto him all nations, and heapeth unto him all people" (Hab. 2:5).

There has been a tendency to look for a United States of Europe, out of which would come Antichrist. That is not quite what Daniel saw. The clay in the image means that those countries can *not* get together, so that every future attempt to unite Europe will fail, as it has always done. The kingdom of Antichrist will not produce the man; the man will produce the kingdom. The man will come first and will gather unto him all nations; he will start with just one country, a small but potentially strong one, and then will take three more by force. The rest will yield to him or else will naturally be on his side.

THE SAME HORN MADE WAR

I beheld, and the same horn made war with the saints, and prevailed against them; until the Ancient of days came, and judgment was given to the saints of the most High; and the time came that the saints possessed the kingdom.

Thus he said, The fourth beast shall be the fourth kingdom. . . diverse from all kingdoms, . . . Out of this kingdom . . . ten kings . . . shall arise: and another shall rise after them; . . . diverse from the first, and he shall subdue three kings. And he shall speak great words against the most High, and shall wear out the saints of the most High, and think to change times and laws: and they shall be given into his hand until a time and times and the dividing of time.

—Dan. 7:21–25.

The same horn. Daniel is very emphatic about one thing: This little horn that comes up out of the midst of the ten is the very same one that persecutes the saints until judgment is given to them and the time comes that they possess the kingdom. We are still paralleling the Revelation story.

Jesus must have had these events in mind when He said, "This generation shall not pass, till all these things be fulfilled" (Matt. 24:34). The generation that will be here when these things start will not pass until they are all fulfilled. They will all come in one generation so that the same horn that will rise and begin this series of events will exist to the end. There will be a mysterious death and resurrection when Satan enters into him, but it will be the same little horn. The same man who will build the new empire (the only one ever to come out of Europe) will be the very one who will come against Christ at the battle of Armageddon. From the rise of this man to the return of Christ in glory will be less than one generation.

The same horn made war with the saints, and prevailed against them. This same statement is made in Revelation: "It was given unto him to *make war with the saints*, and to overcome them" (Rev. 13:7). A question might arise as to why the saints' persecution is recorded in Revelation Chapter 13, whereas in earlier chapters their death and their arrival in heaven is found (chapters 6 and 7). This could be answered by the simple observation that the earlier chapters (chapters 4 to 11) are chronological, and the events are numbered, but the later chapters (chapters 12 to 18) are topical. They cover the same time, but Chapters 12 to 15 are discussed by topics and from a different viewpoint. (A topic may cover the whole time or any part of it.)

In the interpretation of Revelation Chapter 13, there has developed some confusion which could have been avoided by the most cursory investigation—as simple as reading the marginal rendering in any good Bible. The confusion has been caused by a misunderstanding of Revelation 13:5: "There was given unto him a mouth speaking great things and blasphemies; and power was given unto him to continue forty and two months." The marginal rendering of "to continue 42 months" is "to *make war* 42 months." Thus "to continue" is the same word as "to make," used in verse 7. There it is explained, "It was given unto him *to make war with* the saints, and to overcome them." The 42 months (or 3½ years) is not the length of the reign of the beast, the little horn; it is the length of time that he persecutes the saints.

This "beast out of the sea" *must* be the little horn of Daniel, because the beast is the one that has the mouth speaking great things and that persecutes the saints. The beast's kingdom is the subject of the judgment, and the beast is the one that is put down at the coming of Christ (Rev. 19:19, 20).*

There could not be two such persons. Daniel says it is the same one all the way through. He is Antichrist; he will reign more than 3½ years; Daniel says he will confirm the covenant for 7 years. Before he confirmed the covenant, he would have to be in power, so his total reign would have to be more than 7 years. The length of his reign is not given because that would tell the date of the Rapture.

Until the Ancient of days came, and judgment was given to the saints of the most High. This is not a reference to the Second Coming of Christ but to the Ancient of Days coming to His judgment throne that both Daniel and John saw being set up in the sky. The resurrected saints are the executors of this judgment. "Do ye not know that the saints will judge the world?" (I Cor. 6:2).

Against the most High. There has been a rather widespread teaching that the word *antichrist* means "like Christ," and that therefore Antichrist will be a false messiah. Coupled

---

*And I saw the beast, and the kings of the earth, and their armies, gathered together to make war against him that sat on the horse, and against his army. And the beast was taken, and with him the false prophet that wrought miracles before him, with which he deceived them that had received the mark of the beast, and them that worshipped his image. These both were cast alive into a lake of fire burning with brimstone. —Rev. 19:19, 20.

with this, and bearing upon it, is the argument as to whether the beast out of the sea is the false prophet or Antichrist.

These arguments are somewhat on the foolish side because the only places the word *antichrist* appears are in First and Second John, and there antichrist is shown to be anyone who denies Christ. Today, we have taken the word *antichrist* out of its context and arbitrarily applied it to a man that is called by other names in the Bible. I apply the term *Antichrist* to the little horn who is mentioned by many prophets and who is the beast out of the sea in Revelation. If someone else wants to apply the word *antichrist* to a personage mentioned directly only in Revelation, that is his privilege. Each of the prophets has his own name for this man. The term *Antichrist* is more useful if applied to the one talked about in many places in both the Old and New Testaments rather than to one distinctly mentioned only in Revelation.

The word *antichrist* can mean either "like Christ" or "against Christ," for the prefix *anti* has both meanings. The meaning would have to be determined by the context. Certainly in John's vocabulary, it does not mean "like Christ," and what it means in any other vocabulary does not make any difference because the word is not used by any other Bible writer. The little horn is *against* God, *against* Christ, and *against* the saints. No matter by what name he is called, there is not a single statement anywhere in Scripture that says or suggests that the little horn is an imitator of Christ or a false messiah. If he comes *in his own name,* he could not be a false Christ.

In the satanic trinity, the beast is "opposite to" Christ. It is in that sense that he is antichrist. He could not persecute the saints who confess Christ and claim at the same time to be Christ or to be like Christ. None of the beast's recorded actions remind us of Christ. When the world worships him, they will not think they are worshipping Christ. They will be worshipping Satan. *"They worshipped the dragon* which gave power unto the beast, and they worshipped the beast saying: Who is like unto the beast and who is able to make war with him?"

The little horn's ability to make war is demonstrated when he pulls up three horns by the roots. Evidently they are supported by a tremendous power which melts away before the little horn. As Habakkuk says, "He scoffeth at kings, and princes are a derision unto him: he derideth every stronghold; for he heapeth up dust, and taketh it" (Hab. 1:10, R.V.).

And wear out the saints of the most High and think to change times and laws. The saints who are worn out by Antichrist are the ones who are saved after the Resurrection. They are from every kindred, tongue, people, and nation. Before their resurrection they are spoken of as being *under the altar.* "When he had opened the fifth seal, I saw under the altar the souls of them that were slain for the word of God, and for the testimony which they held" (Rev. 6:9). The slain were told that they would have to wait until the others should be killed as they were. Then in Chapter 7 we see that the total number who were raised from the dead and entered heaven was "a great multitude." When Christ comes to reign, these tribulation saints will return with Christ along with the others. They are included in the first Resurrection.

"And I saw thrones, and they sat upon them, and judgment was given unto them" (Rev. 20:4). These are the thrones that Daniel saw set up. These saints are those who are caught up or raised at the Rapture. They are the elders, living ones, horsemen, and angels, who carry out the instructions which proceed from the throne as the seals are broken.

> And I saw the souls of them that were beheaded for the witness of Jesus, and for the word of God, and which had not worshipped the beast, neither his image, neither had received his mark upon their foreheads, or in their hands; and they lived and reigned with Christ

a thousand years.... This is the first resurrection.
                                 —Rev. 20:4, 5.

And think to change times and laws. This is an apt description of a modern dictator. Kings are bound by tradition, and follow the practices of the past. With kings, change comes slowly. But dictators want to change everything at once; in fact, it is the desire for change that brings dictators into power. Every modern dictator has thought to change times and laws. The rise of dictatorship marks a modern trend toward the final dictator. Antichrist will be a dictator rather than a king. In that sense he *shall be diverse from the first.* (This feature is expanded with more detail in a later vision.)

In the original, the word *laws* ("think to change laws") is singular, possibly referring to the basic law of God. The little horn will have no respect for right and wrong, as commonly accepted, but will set up his own standards. For instance, it will be considered right to kill Christians.

3½ YEARS TRIBULATION FOR THE SAINTS*

And they shall be given into his hand. It is usually thought to be the saints that will be given into Antichrist's hand, for they are the ones he will persecute and overcome. The saints are the subjects of this passage. In a very special sense they are "given into his hand." Paul explains it quite thoroughly in II Thessalonians 2:7: "The mystery of iniquity doth already work: only *he who now letteth will let,* until he be taken out of the way." The word *let* is an old English word meaning "to hinder." The Revised Version is better: "The mystery of lawlessness doth already work: only *there is one that restraineth now,* until he be taken out of the way."

Satan is the lawless one, the one who, when he finally gets the opportunity, will think to change the law of God and make right what God says is wrong. He cannot do that

---

* See chart—page 73.

now, for there is one that hinders now—the Holy Spirit working in the Church. Satan does not now have the power to kill all Christians or to change times and laws.

But after the Resurrection when Satan is cast down to the earth, the Holy Spirit will be taken out of the way and will no longer hinder Satan. This will give Satan complete control of the world for the first time, as far as the Spirit's hindrance is concerned. Satan will be hindered by other means—physical means—such as falling stars, earthquakes, fire, etc. This will be the day of Satan's judgment. When the Church is taken out of the way, iniquity will abound; it will come to its harvest.

In II Thessalonians 2:2 Paul is saying that the spirit of iniquity is here now, but can go only so far, for it is held in check by the operation of the Holy Spirit in the Church. But during the reign of Antichrist, after the Resurrection, there will be no such check. Evil will ripen. The judgment will be harvest. "Let them both grow together *until the harvest*." Iniquity will be allowed to develop to its fullest extent, preparatory to judgment.

The only protest against this harvest of evil will be the tribulation saints, so that all the intensity of the wrath of Satan will be directed at them. Then Satan will not be hindered in his wrath, as he is today—for the tribulation saints will be given into his hand for "a time, times, and dividing of time."

Please note that it does *not* say, as some read it, that the Holy Spirit will be taken out of *the world* and go up with the Church. The Holy Spirit is not taken out of the world but out of *the way*. In a wonderful way the Holy Spirit will be with those tribulation saints, and through Him they will be saved. The Holy Spirit will not be taken out of the world. He will merely be taken out of the way of Antichrist.

> And it shall come to pass afterward, that I will pour out my spirit upon all flesh; and your sons and

your daughters shall prophesy, your old men shall dream dreams, your young men shall see visions: and also upon the servants and upon the handmaids in those days will I pour out my spirit.

And I will shew wonders in the heavens and in the earth, blood, and fire, and pillars of smoke. The sun shall be turned into darkness, and the moon into blood, before the great and the terrible day of the Lord come.
—Joel 2:28–31.

Until time, times, and the dividing of time is a symbolic way of saying that the saints will be given into Antichrist's hand for 3½ years. This period of time is stated symbolically and then is explained in order that it would not be possible to make it read 1260 *years*. Some make it read "years" anyway. (Whenever a symbol is explained, the explanation is literal.)

In Revelation 12 and 13, this same period of time is stated three ways and seems, therefore, to have considerable importance. Revelation first speaks of *"a time, and times, and half a time"* (Rev. 12:14). This would be one year, plus two years, plus half a year—that is, 3½ years. In Revelation 12:6 it is stated: "The woman fled into the wilderness, where she hath a place prepared of God, that they should feed her there *a thousand two hundred and threescore days"* (1260 days). That this passage means 1260 years and not days might be argued if it were not for the fact we just mentioned that the time is also stated symbolically in Revelation 12:14. Then to make doubly sure, it is given in Chapter 13:5 as *42 months*.

It is not necessary to make the 3½ years of the tribulation of the saints a part of Daniel's 70th "week" of seven years. It is true that Daniel's week is divided in the midst and that a half of 7 is 3½ years, so that Daniel's 70th week is divided into two parts of 3½ years each. But this 3½ year period of tribulation has to do with the saints, and Daniel's 70th week has to do with the Jews. There is no connection between the two tribulations. The fact that they are the same length (3½ years) does not necessarily mean that they come at the same time. Furthermore, there could be more than one period of 3½ years, or more than two such periods. It is more logical to separate the two periods and more in harmony with the Scriptures. The Bible does not connect this 3½ years with either half of Daniel's 70th week, and there is no reason we should go beyond that which is revealed.

THE JUDGMENT OF THE LITTLE HORN

But the judgment shall sit, and they shall take away his dominion, to consume and to destroy it unto the end.
—Dan. 7:26.

There is one very significant truth demonstrated in Daniel Chapter 7. From the time of the rise of the little horn, heaven as well as earth is in prophetic view, and Daniel passes continually from one to the other. Everything that happens on earth has its counterpart or answer in heaven. This is the case only *after* the rise of the little horn; before his rise, all action is on the earth.

This feature of prophecy (earthly action having its counterpart in heaven) should be better understood. It is well developed in Revelation where both heaven and earth are continually in view. There is a very definite reason for including both, because at the time of the Resurrection, the saints are caught up into heaven and will operate from heaven. They are the principal actors in the Revelation story.

In Revelation we have two sets of circumstances: (1) things that happen in heaven and have a result on the earth— the breaking of the seals, the blowing of trumpets, or pouring out of vials; (2) things that happen on the earth with an instant reaction in heaven—the revelation of the man of sin, and the entrance of Satan personally into the earthly scene.

The judgment shall sit. This is the "day of the Lord." The judgment will sit in heaven; the results will be instantly felt on the earth. Both scenes are constantly in view, heaven and earth. The things that are happening in heaven are just as literal and real as those that are happening on earth. The judgment thrones have been set up in heaven where there is great activity.

This depicting of the heavenly and earthly scenes seems to have confused some expositors. They have treated these heavenly things as symbols of something on the earth, whereas they are actual, literal scenes in heaven. The redemption of the earth is a terrific undertaking and will require the services of all the saints, and of how many angels we do not know. The book of Revelation tells the story as it develops in heaven; the saints are there from every kindred, tongue, people, and nation; the judgment is set; the thrones are occupied; the saints are organized; there are groups of specialists; the heavenly cherubim go into action. There are the elders, the living ones, horsemen, and angels or messengers. Christ is in command, and He breaks the seals. Action follows—always starting in heaven and reaching the earth.

These developments are not symbols; they are real but in heaven. Revelation simply continues the story of the Church *after* the Resurrection. The scene changes to heaven because the saints have been caught up into heaven. Thus Revelation is a continuation of the book of Acts, and follows the course of the Church through the ages. Then when the Resurrection comes, Revelation follows the saints into heaven and continues the story from there. If we insist on treating these heavenly things as symbols of something on the earth, how are we ever going to understand them?

As soon as the Resurrection has taken place, there are two places of interest: heaven and earth. The battle of the earth will be on in earnest, for Satan will be cast out of his present vantage point in the heavens down to the earth. The saints will move in, occupy Satan's old place in heaven, and continue the battle with a terrific bombardment of Satan's kingdom.

The saints will preach the everlasting gospel to every nation and people. In spite of Satan's persecution, a host which no man can number, out of all nations and kindreds and people and tongues, will be saved. Then will come the systematic destruction of Satan's dominion. They (the saints) will destroy it unto the end (Dan. 7:26). The saints will judge the earth.

The book of Daniel, like the book of Revelation, has both heaven and earth in view after the Resurrection, so that all the way through Daniel Chapter 7, the scene is continually shifting from earth to heaven and back again.

The little horn and his movements are given to us in such detail that when he comes, it will not be hard to recognize him. He will fulfill all the prophecy. It was not so with Hitler—he had the demoniac eyes and the mouth speaking great things, and had his origin in the right place; but he did *not* pull up three horns by the roots nor restore the empire in any sense.

Objections have been raised to this clear Bible teaching.

Objection One: Some say we cannot have the saints *in heaven* while others are being saved *on earth* because that would divide the body of Christ—some on the earth and some in heaven.

This strikes me as being rather silly. It is a purely human argument with no support from Scripture. Are not Moses and Elijah a part of the body of Christ? They have gone before us and appeared in their immortal bodies at the transfiguration of Christ. Is not Christ the head of the body? He ascended into heaven. One of the angels that showed the visions to John said he was one of John's fellowservants. In the spirit world, what is the difference between heaven and earth, or between California and New York? What is distance in the spirit world? How far apart do you have to be to be "separated"? Jesus said that He shall "send his angels, and shall gather together his elect from the four winds, from the uttermost part of the *earth* to the uttermost part of *heaven*" (Mark 13:27).

Objection Two: How can people be saved *after* the Rapture when the Dispensation of Grace has ended?

The Bible does not say that the Dispensation of Grace will end with the Rapture. It does say that the tribulation saints will be included in the first Resurrection. It may be that the Dispensation of Grace will end with the Resurrection of the tribulation saints. That would be 3½ years after the Rapture. After the Rapture Daniel's 70th week properly begins. After the Rapture the twelve tribes are first mentioned. No matter who says it, we do not have to believe anything that is not in the Bible.

Objection Three: How can people be saved *after* the Holy Spirit has been taken out of the world?

To answer this, you merely have to quote II Thessalonians 2:7. It says the Spirit will be taken not out of the world but out of the way of the man of sin, so that iniquity may come to a head. When the teachings of men have no Scriptural support, or when men misquote Scripture, we do not have to accept them. Any teaching that is not found in the Bible *could* be wrong, for the Bible is the only source of reliable prophetic information. Only those things that are taught in the Bible are worth considering.

AN EVERLASTING KINGDOM

The kingdom and dominion, and the greatness of the kingdom under the whole heaven, shall be given to the people

of the saints of the most High, whose kingdom is an everlasting kingdom, and all dominions shall serve and obey him.
—Dan. 7:27.

The kingdom shall be given to the people of the saints of the most High. This is not the kingdom of David, which is everlasting too but is limited to a strip from the river of Egypt on the south to the Euphrates on the north, the land over which Abraham traveled. The kingdom of Daniel 7:14 is *under the whole heaven.* It has no limitations. The kingdom of David is a part of it, one of the dominions that will serve Him (Christ). Of the kingdom of heaven, Daniel says in verse 14, "There was given unto him dominion, and glory, and a kingdom, that all people, nations, and languages, should serve him."

During the millennium, the Lord will reign from Jerusalem. This will give Israel great world power, but there will be many other nations. Christ and the saints will reign a thousand years. This thousand years is not the total length of their reign but only the length of time that Satan is chained. The thousand years is the last of seven dispensations, and it will come to an end. Then there will be changes as there have been at the end of all dispensations.

One of the changes will be a shift in the seat of government. The new Holy City will come down out of heaven from God and be the "long home" of the saints and the place from which they reign (Rev. 22:5).* There will still be earthly nations and earthly thrones. The kingdom of David will still have its throne in Jerusalem, and David will reign (Hosea 3:5§; Jer. 30:9¶; Ezek. 37:24, 25**).

*And there shall be no night there; and they need no candle, neither light of the sun; for the Lord God giveth them light: and they shall reign for ever and ever. —Rev. 22:5.

§ Afterward shall the children of Israel return, and seek the Lord their God, and David their king; and shall fear the Lord and his goodness in the latter days.
—Hosea 3:5.

¶ But they shall serve the Lord their God, and David their king, whom I will raise up unto them. —Jer. 30:9.

** And David my servant shall be king over them; and they all shall have one shepherd: they shall also walk in my judgments, and observe my statutes, and

However, this kingdom of David will be only one of the dominions in the kingdom of heaven over which the saints will reign from the Holy City. Christ will reign over the house of Jacob forever, and "of his kingdom there shall be no end." He will be given the throne of His father, David, and will reign in person for one thousand years and from the Holy City forever. When the seat of all government shifts to the Holy City, the earthly throne will be occupied by David, but Christ will still be King of kings. Christ's kingdom will last eternally and will go on increasing forever. "Of the increase of his government and peace there shall be no end" (Isa. 9:7).

The kingdom of heaven is the kingdom of all heaven, *under the whole heaven* (7:27). The Holy City will be its capital because the throne of God will be there. This important verse we are studying (Dan. 7:27) is the connecting link between two eternities. In the eternal past, Lucifer fell and became Satan, and a great expanse of the heavens was brought under his corrupting influence. One-third of the angels might well inhabit one-third of the heavens. That "all" ends with the verse, "The judgment shall sit" (vs. 26). But another eternity begins—a new order, a new kingdom, with a new reigning class, redeemed from the earth, which, from this point, will expand until it has included all that was once Satan's, and then go on increasing forever. There will be a new heaven as well as a new earth. There will be no end to the increase. "A little one shall become a thousand, and a small one a strong nation: I the Lord will hasten it in his time" (Isa. 60:22).

do them. And they shall dwell in the land that I have given unto Jacob my servant, wherein your fathers have dwelt; and they shall dwell therein, even they, and their children, and their children's children for ever: and my servant David shall be their prince for ever. —Ezek. 37:24, 25.

Study 6

DANIEL'S THIRD VISION OF WORLD-EMPIRE

THE COMING OF ANTICHRIST
Daniel 8

THE COMING OF ANTICHRIST
Daniel 8

The rise of the Antichrist is one of the most important subjects in prophecy, and yet it is the most difficult to comprehend. This difficulty is caused by the fact that it involves situations and conditions never before experienced. For this reason our conceptions and therefore our expositions are inadequate. When we enter the realm of Antichrist, we feel that something has been added—there is a fourth dimension which, for want of a better name, we may call "outer space." While the earth is preparing for a conquest of outer space, outer space is preparing for a conquest of the earth.

Space, then, is not a vacuum; it is teeming with life. Scientists debate the question of life on other planets, assuming that life can exist only where there are conditions similar to those on earth. But life in outer space is the kind of life that can exist in outer space. Therefore we do not have to have the same conditions; we only have to have a different kind of being. In outer space, beings are not necessarily friendly. Satan has principalities and powers—organized governments. The satanic conquest of the earth has been, for the most part, a spiritual battle. At the end of the age the added feature is that the battle becomes physical. Then Satan will have a personal representative on the earth who will operate with satanic and therefore supernatural power. This supernatural power is sensationally demonstrated by his ability to make war easily and successfully against the most advanced weapons man can devise—even push-button intercontinental missiles, nuclear weapons, or weapons based in space. The greater *man's* potential for destruction, the more amazing will be Antichrist's almost single-handed accomplishment.

In this chapter we are concerned with Daniel's account of the coming of Antichrist. Some of these features are developed more fully in other Scriptures.

VISION OF THE RAM AND HE-GOAT

The Babylonian Empire—Its End

In the third year of the reign of king Belshazzar a vision appeared unto me, even unto me Daniel, after that which appeared unto me at the first. —Dan. 8:1.

At the time of this chapter, we are nearing the end of the Babylonian Empire. Its last reigning monarch was Belshazzar, in whose short reign Babylon, the head of gold, was to be weighed and found wanting. In the language of Chapter 7, the lion (Babylon) is about to give place to the bear (Persia).

The visions of Daniel concern the future, not the past; therefore, after the Babylonian Empire had actually passed into history, Daniel began his new prophecy with the new empire, Persia. As always, the purpose of this new vision (ch. 8) is to add details not found in the earlier ones (chs. 2 and 7).

Now concerning the new symbols of Chapter 8, it is well to remember that all symbols and parables follow a pattern. They are never strained to cover more ground than they are naturally capable of doing. Instead, a new parable or symbol is employed. This principle is well illustrated in the New Testament in the parables of the kingdom, where there is a separate parable for each separate truth. The same kingdom is likened to seed, to buried treasure, to a pearl, or to fish in a net. These widely different symbols are used to illustrate different phases of the same thing. Symbols are limited in their application and must not be carried beyond their natural function; instead, new symbols are employed to express new features.

This is also Daniel's method. In Chapter 8 the bear of the previous vision becomes a ram; the leopard, a goat. The beast of Chapter 7 does not appear except in its final form. The *first* vision (ch. 2) emphasized Babylon and the Kingdom of heaven; the *second* vision (ch. 7) passed over Babylon and Persia and Greece with one verse each, but specialized on the fourth empire—the Roman Empire. The *third* vision (ch. 8) fills in details about the Persian and Grecian Empires, but, note carefully, it skips entirely the Roman Empire, except for the little horn. Each symbol is not strained to cover any more than it can do naturally. All the visions culminate with either the establishing of the Kingdom or the destruction of Antichrist (which is actually the same thing).

Although symbols are changed in order to bring into view new features and events, there is always enough similarity so that they can be easily identified. For instance, the numerical note of the second world-empire is the figure *two*. (The image had two arms; the bear, two sides; and the ram, two horns.) The numerical note of the third empire is the figure *four*. (The leopard had four wings; the goat grew four horns.) Then, too, the fourth empire had *iron* legs and the *iron* teeth. The emergence of the final Antichrist is symbolized by a "little horn."

The Ram—The Persian Empire

And I saw in a vision; and it came to pass, when I saw, that I was at Shushan in the palace, which is in the province

of Elam; and I saw in a vision, and I was by the river of Ulai.

Then I lifted up mine eyes, and saw, and, behold, there stood before the river a ram which had two horns: and the two horns were high; but one was higher than the other, and the higher came up last. —Dan. 8:2, 3.

The province of Elam, where Daniel was when he saw the vision, was east of the city of Babylon across the Euphrates and Tigris Rivers. The ram corresponds to the bear that got up, first on one side and then the other (ch. 7). The Persian Empire, which was to conquer Babylon, was made up of two countries: Media, with its ancient people, and Persia, with its more modern tribe. Therefore it was called the Medo-Persian Empire.

Symbols are always explained by some means. For instance, the first of the four parts of the image was explained to Nebuchadnezzar by Daniel: *"Thou* art this head of gold." Again we have in Chapter 8 a positive statement as to the identity of the second kingdom: "The ram which thou sawest having two horns *are the kings of Media and Persia"* (Dan. 8: 20). "King" is often used in place of kingdom, and so the symbol may be applied either to the king, or to the kingdom, or to both. In Daniel 2: 39 Nebuchadnezzar is told, "After thee shall arise another kingdom inferior to thee."

Expansion Northwest

I saw the ram pushing westward, and northward, and southward; so that no beast might stand before him, neither was there any that could deliver out of his hand; but he did according to his will, and became great. —Dan. 8:4.

The expansion of empire in those days was always toward the west, north, and to some extent, south. This general direction of conquest continued until all southern

Europe was included, right to the Atlantic Ocean. This is an interesting note, inasmuch as in the last days the direction of movement will be in the reverse until Babylon, Persia, and Elam are again segments of a world-empire.

The Goat—The Grecian Empire

And as I was considering, behold, an he goat came from the west on the face of the whole earth, and touched not the ground: and the goat had a notable horn between his eyes. And he came to the ram that had two horns, which I had seen standing before the river, and ran unto him in the fury of his power.

And I saw him come close unto the ram, and he was moved with choler against him, and smote the ram, and brake his two horns: and there was no power in the ram to stand before him, but he cast him down to the ground, and stamped upon him: and there was none that could deliver the ram out of his hand.

Therefore the he goat waxed very great: and when he was strong, the great horn was broken; and for it came up four notable ones toward the four winds of heaven.

—Dan. 8:5–8.

Here the numerical notes that connect with the other visions are the figures *one* and *four*. *One* connects with the image—the trunk of the image was one as contrasted with the arms, legs, and toes. *Four* connects with the four wings and four heads of the leopard.

Again we have the inspired interpretation of the details. "And *the rough goat is the king of Grecia*: and the great *horn* that is between his eyes *is the first king*" (Dan. 8:21). The *"first king"* of Greece was Alexander the Great. He made swift conquest of the world, defeated the Persians, and became a world-ruler. However, when the empire of Alexander reached its greatest extent, the young conqueror fell victim of his own excesses and died. At his death there was great confusion, and a number of men who tried to take over the empire were slain. Finally, the empire was divided into four parts ("four notable ones"), each with a separate ruler. They were 1) Macedonia and Greece; 2) Asia Minor; 3) Syria; 4) Cyrene.

Division of Alexander's Empire

Its Little Horn—Antichrist

And out of one of them came forth a little horn, which waxed exceeding great, toward the south, and toward the east, and toward the pleasant land. —Dan. 8:9.

The little horn. Up to this point the commentators are pretty much in agreement; but from this point on, difficulties multiply. It will, therefore, be necessary to stick closely to the rules of interpretation and let the Scriptures interpret themselves. There are many textual difficulties, but the modern versions agree substantially with the Authorized Version. In place of *pleasant* land, we read "beauteous land," or "glorious land"; but in any case the reference would have to be to Palestine.

The interpretation revolves around the identity of "the little horn." With one accord the commentators say the little horn is Antiochus Epiphanes. It is true he persecuted the Jews in Palestine but not to the extent of Hitler's persecution. Antiochus did *not* fulfill the prophecy, or any part of it. It is said that he put a sow in the temple and caused the Jews to worship it. This is said to be "the transgression of desolation" mentioned in the thirteenth verse.

Daniel mentions "the abomination of desolation" a number of times (9:27; 11:31; 12:11), always in reference to Antichrist. In the Olivet Discourse Jesus said, "When ye therefore shall see *the abomination of desolation,* spoken of by Daniel, the prophet, standing in the holy place. . . ." Then Jesus goes on to tell about the signs of His coming again. Here Jesus referred to this "abomination of desolation" as something future, not past. He connected it with the persecution of the Jews by Antichrist, not Antiochus. Antiochus does *not* appear in prophecy. His acts had no prophetic significance and no lasting results. In importance he does not approach Adolph Hitler, whose persecutions do have prophetic significance and lasting results—he forced the Jews to return to Palestine— and so for the first time since Daniel, we have an independent Jewish state.

Please refer again to the Harmony Chart of Daniel's visions (pages 112, 113). Although in the different visions the symbols may differ, there are always points of contact and of similarities, so that the various parts may be readily identified. This is done by the use of numbers and descriptive words. If, then, we find in two successive visions such a highly descriptive term as "little horn," it would have to refer to the same thing in both places, or we have no basis for interpretation.

In the Harmony Chart you will notice that the little horn of Daniel 8 appears in the same relative position as the little horn of Daniel 7, not only in reference to the other visions of Daniel, but also in Revelation, the Olivet Discourse, and others. The stone was cut out "without hand," and the little horn is destroyed "without hand." All of the visions end with the destruction of Antichrist. This little horn follows this pattern exactly. The value of the Harmony Chart is that you can see the whole picture at once. Note how each part fits into the whole so that an erroneous interpretation can instantly be detected.

We also have an inspired explanation of the vision of Chapter 8. An angel appeared on purpose to explain the meaning to Daniel and said, "Gabriel, make this man to understand the vision. So he came near where I stood: . . . he said unto me, Understand, O son of man" (vs. 16, 17). So we follow here the explanation of the angel rather than that of the commentaries. When the angel says, "he shall also stand up against the Prince of princes; but he shall be broken without hand," the angel is talking about the little horn. This statement could not be said of anybody else. Moreover, it follows the pattern of all the visions. It is not consistent or even reasonable to make the *symbol*, "the little horn," apply to Antiochus and the *explanation* of the symbol to Antichrist. If Antiochus did not fulfill the symbol and in no way connects with the explanation of the symbol, he should be completely excluded from our thinking.

Chapter 8 skips from the third empire to the focal point of all the visions—the rise of Antichrist. (Details of the fourth empire, however, are found in the previous vision— Chapter 7.) Note carefully that these visions cover 2,500 years of time. Many years have to be passed over with only a passing remark. The phrase in Chapter 8 that carries us across the more than 2,000 years is this: "In the latter time of their kingdom" (vs. 23). The little horn, we are told, is to come out of one of the four winds of heaven (vs. 8). Which wind it is, is immediately indicated: he will wax great toward the south, east, and toward Palestine. To do this, he will have to start in the north and west. The previous vision says that the little horn will conquer three countries of the Roman Empire. In the next vision, Daniel mentions the restoration of the kingdom, referring to the Roman Empire. In Revelation, the beast has ten horns, indicating again the Roman Empire.

Geopolitics

In the first vision (ch. 2) the ten horns appeared as ten toes, ten nations that came out of the Roman Empire, and of them Daniel said, "In the days of these kings shall the God of heaven set up a kingdom" (2:44). The nucleus of Antichrist's kingdom will be the Roman Empire. To obtain this kingdom, he must wax great in three directions: south, east, and toward Palestine.

"The share of the earth controlled by each nation is a matter involving geography as well as government." In modern times, this principle has been developed into a science called geopolitics, which "is concerned with the dependence of the domestic and foreign politics of a people upon physical environment." Geopolitics was known in Germany by the Kaiser, and he based his hopes of world domination on it. But not until the end of World War I was the theory of geopolitics developed into a science and put into print. It then become the first principle of all would-be world conquerors. It has three basic principles:

1. Who rules East Europe commands the Heartland (the Middle East).
2. Who rules the Heartland commands the World-Island (Palestine).
3. Who rules the World-Island commands the world.

Thus, he who rules East Europe commands the Middle East, commands Palestine, commands the world. (See the *Encyclopedia Britannica* under Geopolitics and Sir Halford Mackinder.) In 1919 Sir Halford Mackinder wrote:

> In a monkish map contemporary with the Crusades and which still hangs in Herford Cathedral, Jerusalem is marked as at the geographical center, the navel of the world; and on the floor of the Church of the Holy Sepulchre at Jerusalem they will show to this day the precise spot which is the center.
>
> If our study of the geographical realities as we now know them in their completeness is leading us to right conclusions, the medieval ecclesiastics were not far wrong.
>
> If the World-Island be inevitably the principal seat of humanity on this globe, and if Arabia, as the passage-land from Europe to the Indies and from the northern to the southern Heartland, be central in the World-Island, then the hill citadel of Jerusalem has a strategical position with reference to world realities not differing essentially from its ideal position in the perspective of the Middle Ages.

Sir Halford saw the United States, Britain, Japan and other great nations as mere satellites of the dictator who held control of the World-Island. Palestine has always been a World-Island, and will be until the "law shall go forth of Zion, and the word of the Lord from Jerusalem." The prophets knew about the World-Island. Now that all world action is centering in those lands, a great mass of prophecy is on the verge of fulfillment.

Acting on this theory, Russia captured and still holds three countries of East Europe. Before and during the reign of Antichrist, the Middle East (the Heartland) will be the scene of the most violent activity. This activity is the subject of the next vision (ch. 11). The final world battle, called Armageddon, is an attempt on the part of all nations to get control of Palestine or to prevent Christ and the saints from taking over that land.

Palestine always has been an island surrounded by ene-mies. It is becoming a World-Island. All conquerors recog-nize it as such. This fact was well known to the prophets. "Who commands the World-Island rules the world," says the author of geopolitics. Isaiah said the same thing:

> And it shall come to pass in the last days, that the mountain of the Lord's house shall be established in the top of the mountains, and shall be exalted above the hills; and all nations shall flow unto it. And many people shall go and say, Come ye, and let us go up to the mountain of the Lord, to the house of the God of Jacob; and he will teach us of his ways, and we will walk in his paths: for out of Zion shall go forth the law, and the word of the Lord from Jerusalem.
> —Isa. 2:2, 3.

Antichrist will follow the same course. He will move toward the east and toward Palestine. He will take East Europe. If Russia still holds it, he will defeat Russia. From the very beginning he will aim at Palestine. He will not make military conquest of Palestine until the time of Armageddon and then it will be too late. (This story is told in the next vision, ch. 11.)

Next in Chapter 8:10–14 we have a scene that has been called the most difficult passage in prophecy. It would be if you are thinking about Antiochus Epiphanes. However, the prophet is talking about something vastly different from any-thing that happened historically between the time of the Old and New Testaments. This passage may be difficult, but it is extremely important. It contains the one element of mystery that makes the rise of Antichrist so much different from that of any conqueror that has preceded him.

The details of Antichrist's rise are unbelievable before they happen because Antichrist has his roots in outer space. God expressed this truth to Habakkuk: "Behold ye among the heathen [nations], and regard, and wonder marvelously, for I will work a work in your days, which ye will not believe, though it be told you" (Hab. 1:5).

Satan Takes Over

And it waxed great, even to the host of heaven; and it cast down some of the host and of the stars to the ground, and stamped upon them. Yea, he magnified himself even to the prince of the host, and by him the daily sacrifice was taken away, and the place of his sanctuary was cast down.

And an host was given him against the daily sacrifice by reason of transgression, and it cast down the truth to the ground; and it practised, and prospered.

Then I heard one saint speaking, and another saint said unto that certain saint which spake, How long shall be the vision concerning the daily sacrifice, and the transgression of desolation, to give both the sanctuary and the host to be trodden under foot? And he said unto me, Unto two thousand and three hundred days; then shall the sanctuary be cleansed. —Dan. 8:10–14.

He magnified himself even to the prince of the host. This section has been very difficult to translate; the versions all differ. The Authorized Version is as good as any, but one change should be noted. *The Pulpit Commentary* says of verse eleven: "It is assumed that *the little horn* is the subject of this sentence; but *horn* is feminine in Hebrew, and the verbs here (in verse eleven) are in the masculine; this is against its being the nominative. The *prince of the host*, then, must be the nominative of the verbs and subject of the sentence. The rendering of the first clause ought to be: '*Until the prince of the host magnify himself, and by himself he shall offer the daily sacrifice.*'" Another rendering is: "Until the prince of the host shall *make himself greater [than the little horn]* and shall offer the daily sacrifice." This makes it much easier to understand.

The prince of the host is Satan. Revelation tells of his angels falling from heaven. Satan's great ambition is to be like God, not in perfection but in power and glory. This was the first cause of his downfall (Isa. 14: 12–17).*

At the time of the end Satan will satisfy this consuming desire; he will sit in the temple of God showing himself that he is God (II Thess. 2:4). The abomination of desolation is Satan in the temple mockingly offering the daily sacrifice.

And it waxed great, even to the host of heaven; and it cast down some of the host and of the stars to the ground. The host of heaven are the angels of heaven. Some are called fallen angels because they seem to have participated in the fall of Satan; they are Satan's angels. Sometimes people are surprised to find that these fallen angels are still in heaven. The fall has to do with their moral state, not their place of abode. When the sons of God came to present themselves before the Lord, Satan came also among them (Job 1:6).§

Heaven is a big place; in fact, it may cover all outer space. It is quite certain that the space in the vicinity of the earth is infested by Satan's angels as well as demons of various orders. Prophecy is specific about the fact that the heavens as well as the earth must be cleansed. Both Isaiah¶ and Revelation** speak of the new heaven and the new earth. This cleansing starts in the heavens but is soon transferred to the earth.

Antichrist, whose coming is after the working of Satan, makes contact with the host of heaven. That is when Satan, using the physical properties of Antichrist, becomes a man.

---

* How art thou fallen from heaven, O Lucifer, son of the morning! how art thou cut down to the ground, which didst weaken the nations! For thou hast said in thine heart, I will ascend into heaven, I will exalt my throne above the stars of God: I will sit also upon the mount of the congregation, in the sides of the north: I will ascend above the heights of the clouds; I will be like the most High.
Yet thou shalt be brought down to hell, to the sides of the pit. They that see thee shall narrowly look upon thee, and consider thee, saying, Is this the man that made the earth to tremble, that did shake kingdoms; that made the world as a wilderness, and destroyed the cities thereof; that opened not the house of his prisoners? —Isa. 14:12–17.

§ Now there was a day when the sons of God came to present themselves before the Lord, and Satan came also among them. —Job 1:6.

¶ For, behold, I create new heavens and a new earth: and the former shall not be remembered, nor come into mind. —Isa. 65:17.

** And I saw a new heaven and a new earth: for the first heaven and the first earth were passed away; and there was no more sea. —Rev. 21:1.

There is no question that Revelation 12 has reference to the same event as Daniel 8: 10: "His tail drew the third part of the stars of heaven, and did cast them to the earth. . . . And the great dragon was cast out, that old serpent, called the Devil, and Satan, which deceiveth the whole world: he was cast out into the earth, and his angels were cast out with him" (vs. 4, 9). Satan will reign in person on the earth. The little horn will become Satan. How this is accomplished is told in Revelation 13.

Some of the wording here is difficult to translate because it deals with something beyond our comprehension. There are no words for it. This passage, however, is the key to the last days of the age. Scientists may discover the physical characteristics of outer space, but the earth will suddenly come to realize that the heavens are full of living beings who have designs on the earth.

Man is making conquest of outer space, but in so doing, he may be stirring up a nest of hornets. The most devastating realization which the people of the earth will ever experience will come when they suddenly wake up to the fact that, instead of our making conquest of outer space, the beings of outer space are making conquest of the earth. This begins at the temple. Satan, as usual, is following God's pattern, for Jesus started at the temple. After the triumphal entry into Jerusalem, He went immediately to the temple and cleansed it. His coming again will be to the temple first, as far as the Jews are concerned. ("The Lord, whom ye seek, shall suddenly come to his temple." —Mal. 3: 1.) Daniel deals with the coming of Satan as it relates to the nations. Revelation is concerned only with his relationship to the saints.

2300 Days

How long shall be the vision concerning the daily sacrifice, and the transgression of desolation, to give both the sanctuary

and the host to be trodden under foot? And he said unto me, Unto 2300 days; then shall the sanctuary be cleansed. This 2300 days would amount to about 6½ years. There is a 10½ year period between the Rapture and the return of Christ. The last 7 years correspond to Daniel's 70th week. During the first 3½ years, Antichrist is engaged in getting rid of the saints. Then he turns his attention to the Jews. We do not know exactly when these 2300 days start, or where they end. We are informed here only of the total length of time in which the temple will be subject to desecration.

AN INSPIRED EXPLANATION

"The Time of the End"

And it came to pass, when I, even I Daniel, had seen the vision, and sought for the meaning, then, behold, there stood before me as the appearance of a man. And I heard a man's voice between the banks of Ulai, which called, and said, Gabriel, make this man to understand the vision.

So he came near where I stood: and when he came, I was afraid, and fell upon my face: but he said unto me, Understand, O son of man: for at the time of the end shall be the vision.

Now as he was speaking with me, I was in a deep sleep on my face toward the ground: but he touched me, and set me upright. And he said, Behold, I will make thee know what shall be in the last end of the indignation: for at the time appointed the end shall be. —Dan. 8:15–19.

The time of the end, like "the day of the Lord" or "that day," is a reference to the events that lead up to the coming of Christ. This "time" is the focal point of all prophecy. Now and then a prophet gets a glimpse beyond the time of the end and sees something of the new beginning. This is particularly true of Isaiah, and of course of Revelation. But for the most part the prophets concentrated on the events leading up to the Second Coming of Christ and the establishing of the kingdom of heaven. That is the end of things as we know them today.

The dominant world figure at the time of the end is Antichrist, called here "the little horn." Three verses are given to the background, the empires of Persia and Greece.

Persia and Greece

The ram which thou sawest having two horns are the kings of Media and Persia. And the rough goat is the king of Grecia: and the great horn that is between his eyes is the first king. Now that being broken, whereas four stood up for it, four kingdoms shall stand up out of the nation, but not in his power. —Dan. 8:20–22.

King Alexander died suddenly; no provision had been made for his successor. After much confusion, the empire was divided. None of Alexander's sons became a ruler, so his generals took over. Four kings stood up "but not in his power."

Antichrist

And in the latter time of their kingdom, when the transgressors are come to the full, a king of fierce countenance, and understanding dark sentences, shall stand up. And his power shall be mighty, but not by his own power: and he shall destroy wonderfully, and shall prosper, and practise, and shall destroy the mighty and the holy people. —Dan. 8:23, 24.

Let us examine in greater detail these two verses phrase by phrase:

In the latter time of their kingdom. Here we pass by all the years from Alexander to Antichrist and are brought to "the time of the end," as the angel said.

When the transgressors are come to the full. Jesus referred to this particular evil time as "the harvest" (Matt. 13:30).* Harvest is the end of a growing season. The judgment day will be a harvest. God will judge only a finished work. He will allow evil to reach a harvest. "The time of trouble such as never was" (Dan. 12:1) § will be due directly to the time of evil such as never was. But everything will be in its order. The reference to evil here is not to the moral condition of the people but to the spread of bad government. Those who are attempting to enslave the world and whose tactics are violence, lies, confiscation of property and rigged courts, will reach the utmost limit of their potential. This is vividly expressed by Habakkuk, speaking on this same theme:

> O Lord, how long shall I cry, and thou wilt not hear! even cry out unto thee of violence, and thou wilt not save! Why dost thou shew me iniquity, and cause me to behold grievance? for spoiling and violence are before me: and there are that raise up strife and contention. Therefore the law is slacked, and judgment doth never go forth: for the wicked doth compass about the righteous; therefore wrong judgment proceedeth. —Hab. 1:2–4.

When this corruption has become so extensive that the whole world is threatened, then the transgressors have "come to the full." It is to this situation that Jesus referred when He spoke of wars and commotions, and added, "Be not terrified"— indicating the threat not only to world peace but to world safety. The transgressors will have terrifying weapons that will seemingly give them the power to destroy all people.

A king of fierce countenance and understanding dark sentences shall stand up. This is the angel's explana-

---

* Let both grow together until the harvest: and in the time of harvest I will say to the reapers, Gather ye together first the tares, and bind them in bundles to burn them, but gather the wheat into my barn. —Matt. 13:30.

§ And at that time shall Michael stand up, the great prince which standeth for the children of thy people: and there shall be a time of trouble, such as never was since there was a nation even to that same time: and at that time thy people shall be delivered, every one that shall be found written in the book. —Dan. 12:1.

tion of the "little horn." His coming is at a time of world crisis brought on by "the transgressors" (8:23). They not only reach their limits; they exceed their limits. Then something unexpected happens. What is said about Antichrist is not very extensive; but it does go a long way toward filling in the other prophecies. He is prominent in three relationships: to the nations; to the Jews; and to the Church. A harmony of all the references to him could reveal a large amount of information. We have previously noted Antichrist's eyes and mouth. Now we may add "a fierce countenance." His appearence should not be underrated, for it will have a lot to do with his success—or, it may be more accurate to say that the thing that makes him so powerful also gives him his fierce look.

We may have to wait the event to get the full meaning of the phrase "understanding dark sentences." The expression could mean that he deals with familiar spirits or has some kind of demon possession. Paul said his coming is after the working of Satan. He will have a superior knowledge supplied by Satan, which will give him power to cope with every situation, even atomic war.

His power shall be mighty, but not by his own power. Again we are told that the rise of this man is going to be different from anything that has ever happened. That difference lies in the source of his power. It does not come from the science laboratories or from the research plants of industry. He will not have kept up with Russia in the development of atomic warfare, but he will have a certain knowledge that will make him master over anything the nations can produce.

Today, as never before, knowledge is power. Some nation could build up, by long scientific research, a vast system of nuclear warfare, even based in space, so that it could absolutely control every square mile of the earth; and one man, with a superior knowledge, could nullify the whole thing.

Satan has that knowledge. Antichrist will not be impressed by the world's might. A man "whose coming is after the working of Satan" (II Thess. 2:9) and who operates "not by his own power" will laugh at the world's armaments. Habakkuk puts it in these words: "Yea, he scoffeth at kings, and princes are a derision unto him; he derideth every stronghold; for he heapeth up dust and taketh it" (Hab. 1:10, R.V.).

The more formidable the world's weapons, the more sensational will be Antichrist's exploits. They will bring him not only admiration and wonder but actual worship. His association with Satan will not embarrass him, although it will be well-known, at least after the Rapture, for we are told, "The dragon gave him his power, and his seat [throne], and great authority. . . . And they worshipped the dragon which gave power unto the beast: and, they worshipped the beast, saying, Who is like unto the beast? who is able to make war with him?" (Rev. 13:2, 4).

And he shall destroy wonderfully. Young translates this literally: "And wonderful things he destroyeth." To get the full significance of this remarkable prediction, you must recognize certain principles of interpretation. The prophets never exaggerated; nearly all prophecy is understatement. The prophets dealt with extreme cases where exaggeration would be impossible. To cross the ocean the first time on a steamboat might have seemed wonderful. Every great advance of science has had its wonderful aspects. Wonderful things are commonplace today. But none are wonderful enough to fulfill the prophecy, so that we must yet have the most wonderful things that could possibly be realized. When the ultimate comes, prophecy will be ready for fulfillment. We may be justified in believing that we have reached this place in prophetic development when nations have acquired the power to destroy the earth and begin the conquest of space.

The use of the word "destroy" is also significant. The English word destroy is used to translate a large number of

Hebrew words with various meanings. Here, it means to destroy in the literal sense of demolish so that the object can no longer perform its intended function. How up-to-date this sounds—"*destroy wonderfully.*" When the great nations are in a race to find the most wonderful way of destroying, the nation that can be the first to obtain the ultimate weapon will rule the world. The race is on, but it will be Antichrist, not Russia who, in the end, will destroy wonderfully.

Whom will Antichrist destroy? This question may be answered. He will not destroy his own kingdom. Nor will he destroy the nations of the Roman Empire; for concerning them, Daniel said, "In the days of these kings shall the God of heaven set up a kingdom." Also, he will not destroy America. The Philadelphia and Laodicean and other churches are here, and the Laodicean Church at least is rich and increased with goods. This will almost have to be the principal location of the tribulation saints. There is only one nation that would stand in the way of Antichrist. Two conquerors, each with a consuming ambition to rule the world, could not long exist side by side. (The only reason Russia has lasted as long as she has is that she has no competition; no other nation is threatening the whole world.) When "the little horn stands up," everything will change. It will be either the one or the other. It is the little horn who destroys wonderfully.

He shall prosper and practise, and shall destroy the mighty and the holy people. It now becomes necessary for us to orient ourselves by reference to the original vision (which is here being explained) and also by reference to other prophecies.

First, in reference to the vision: "Out of one of them came forth a little horn, which waxed exceeding great, toward the south, and toward the east, and toward the pleasant land" (Dan. 8:9). After Antichrist waxes great toward Palestine, there is a change which is brought about by the injection of spirit forces. Although from the start Satan will empower

Antichrist, the actual presence of satanic beings on the earth will be something this world has never seen. Then Antichrist will begin his war with the saints. We know from Revelation that this follows the Rapture immediately. In this connection we are told that he practiced and prospered (Dan. 8:12). The main feature of this phase of Antichrist's reign is the persecution of the tribulation saints. This puts the time of verses ten to twelve in the middle of verse 24 (verse 24 being the explanation). That is the time when Satan begins to "practice" and to kill the saints. This harmonizes perfectly with Daniel 7 and also with the book of the Revelation.

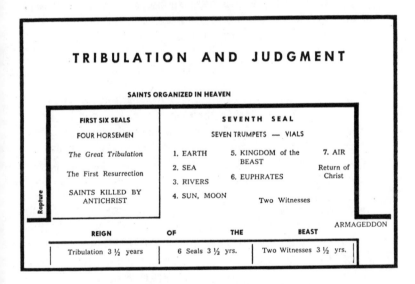

Broken Without Hand

And through his policy also he shall cause craft to prosper in his hand; and he shall magnify himself in his heart, and by peace shall destroy many: he shall also stand up against the Prince of princes: but he shall be broken without hand.
—Dan. 8:25.

By peace [Antichrist] shall destroy many. Two details need to be mentioned here. First, although the versions differ somewhat, they are quite generally agreed in translating *peace* by the word *treachery:* "By treachery shall destroy many." The word also means *suddenly.** If we put this alongside of Daniel 7, we find that the little horn actually takes by force only three other nations of the Roman Empire. The rest of his empire he acquires by craft and treachery. This does not mean that Antichrist will not destroy other countries outside of the Roman Empire. They would not be included in this prophecy.

Second, "he stands up against the Prince of princes." He is *anti*-Christ. The statement here is brief because it is fully developed in parallel accounts.

True But Future

And the vision of the evening and the morning which was told is true: wherefore shut thou up the vision; for it shall be for many days. And I Daniel fainted, and was sick certain days; afterward I rose up, and did the king's business; and I was astonished at the vision, but none understood it.
—Dan. 8:26, 27.

Shut thou up the vision. It was the meaning of the prophecy, not the prophecy itself, that was shut up. The vision was made known, but none understood it. At the time, it had no particular function because its fulfillment was in the distant future. This illustrates one of the most important features of prophecy—its purpose. This is not an isolated case; it goes to the very heart of all prophecy. Except for a few items which were fulfilled at the first advent of Christ and the beginning of the Church, prophecy looks ahead to one period of time, not more than a generation long, in which

---

* Daniel 11:21 supports the Authorized rendering "peace." Antichrist uses peace as an instrument of conquest. The modern term is cold war.

will come the greatest changes of all time. The climax of all the ages is the Second Coming of Christ. It will outclass all the other world crises, such as the Flood, the Tower of Babel, the Exodus from Egypt, and even the miracles of Jesus. The Second Coming of Christ has a feature that was largely lacking in the previous crises—the active participation of the spirit world, or, as we call it, outer space.

I Daniel fainted and was sick. It was not something Daniel ate that caused him to faint, but something he saw. Words in themselves are always inadequate to express a vision. We do not faint when we read what Daniel saw. In the same way, on the Mount of Transfiguration, though the disciples were completely overcome by what they saw, merely reading about it in our day does not give us the same experience. But we may not have long to wait to see the fulfillment of Daniel's vision. If Daniel fainted because he saw a vision of a part of what is going to happen, what will be the experience of those who go through the actual events?

DANIEL'S FOURTH VISION
OF WORLD-EMPIRE

AN ELABORATE INTRODUCTION
Daniel 10

AN ELABORATE INTRODUCTION
Daniel 10

No prophecy in the Bible has a more elaborate introduction than this fourth vision, for all of Daniel Chapter 10 serves but to introduce Chapter 11. These are the most important chapters in Daniel and probably the least understood. Commentaries are almost useless. Some commentators say Chapter 11 should not be in the Bible, but our Harmony Chart shows that it belongs there.

In this fourth vision, instead of symbols we have plain words, but the plain words are harder to understand than the symbols of the three earlier visions; in fact, if we did not have the symbols of the other visions, we would not get much from the plain words. Symbols are an amazing invention when one realizes what is accomplished by them.

The purpose of the fourth vision is not to explain the symbols of the previous visions (these have already been explained), but to give details not covered by the symbols. Symbols are always limited to a narrow field, and therefore we have to keep changing the symbols. A recital of Antichrist's exploits can be a complex matter; therefore details of his movements could not very well be reduced to symbols.

However, we need the symbols of the previous visions. A harmony of all Daniel's visions (see pages 112, 113) also becomes more essential than ever. We must also keep in mind that in this vision more than one event or circumstance may sometimes be under view at one time. Daniel stops now and then to go back and pick up the story from another angle. Though events may be predicted one after the other, they can actually be happening at the same time. Though a football game and a baseball game are being played at the same time, no writer can record the two at the same time. He has to describe first one, then the other. Even so, the prophetic method is to follow the main thought through to the end without deviation, though some important details have to be temporarily omitted; then the prophet goes back and fills in the items left out. This was also the method of Jesus in the Olivet Discourse.

A LONG-TERM VISION

In the third year of Cyrus king of Persia a thing was revealed unto Daniel, whose name was called Belteshazzar; and the thing was true, but the time appointed was long: and he understood the thing, and had understanding of the vision. —Dan. 10:1.

This verse illustrates the difficulties encountered when we leave the symbolical and get into literal language. We would like to take this verse as it appears in the Authorized Version, even though it is in question.

The thing was true but the time appointed was long. Daniel realized he was seeing something that would not happen for a long time, but that fact did not affect its certainty. The Hebrew for "appointed time," *tsaba*, seems to have more than one meaning. Its usual meaning is *warfare*. The Revised Version reads, "The thing was true, even a great warfare." The Masoretic (Jewish Version) reads the same way, although it usually follows the King James very closely. *Young's Literal Translation* reads, "The thing is true, and the warfare is great."

Against this, we have the same Hebrew word, *tsaba,* in Job 7: 1 and 14: 14 translated not "warfare," but "appointed time." In these verses in Job, "appointed time" makes much better sense. "Is there not *an appointed time* to man upon the earth? Are not his days also like the days of an hireling?" When we fit these different meanings of the one Hebrew word into their context in Job, "appointed time," not "warfare," must be the meaning. The same is true of Job 14: 14: "If a man die, shall he live again? all the days of *my appointed time* will I wait, till my change come." Job's days were not all warfare. *Tsaba* is also translated "army," "battle," "company," "host," "service," "soldiers," and "waited upon."

A MAN FROM HEAVEN

Then I lifted up mine eyes, and looked, and behold a certain man clothed in linen, whose loins were girded with fine gold of Uphaz: his body also was like the beryl, and his face as the appearance of lightning, and his eyes as lamps of fire, and his arms and his feet like in colour to polished brass, and the voice of his words like the voice of a multitude. —Dan. 10:5, 6.

After Daniel had fasted and prayed for three weeks, the answer came. The description of the man clothed in linen is strikingly like that of Christ in Revelation 1: 12–17. A point by point comparison will show the following:

Daniel 10: 5, 6	*Revelation* 1: 13–15
A certain man	Like the Son of man
Clothed in linen and girded with gold	Long garment and golden girdle
Body like beryl	(Not mentioned)
Face as the appearance of lightning	(Not mentioned)

Eyes as lamps of fire	Eyes as flames of fire
Feet like polished brass	Feet like burnished brass
Voice like a multitude	Voice like many waters

This resemblance between the two men is too close to be disregarded. Here could be the usual appearance of heavenly beings who are seen by men, or it could have been Christ himself who appeared to Daniel. Though the Revelation description of Christ contains features not seen by Daniel, Daniel saw Christ before His incarnation and resurrection. If we do consider that this angel was Christ himself, then we have to account for the fact that until Michael came to His aid, Satan was able to withstand Him (vs. 13).

GOD ANSWERS PRAYER

He said unto me, O Daniel, a man greatly beloved, understand the words that I speak unto thee, and stand upright: for unto thee am I now sent. And when he had spoken this word unto me, I stood trembling.

Then said he unto me, Fear not, Daniel: for from the first day that thou didst set thine heart to understand, and to chasten thyself before thy God, thy words were heard, and I am come for thy words. But the prince of the kingdom of Persia withstood me one and twenty days: but, lo, Michael, one of the chief princes, came to help me; and I remained there with the kings of Persia. —Dan. 10:11-13.

I am come for thy [Daniel's] words. This vision was an answer to prayer. Only Daniel prayed, and only Daniel saw. Those who were with him felt a quake and fled. Not only was Daniel's prayer heard in heaven, but it was taken seriously there. As a result of his prayer, consultations were held, forces were put into action. To Daniel it seemed like a three weeks' delay, but in heaven there was action all the time. So we are given here a most intimate view of the relationship of heaven and earth, which is much closer than most people realize.

The earth is not only the battleground of the two great forces of the universe; it is also a proving ground for the rulers of future worlds. When we consider that "God so loved the world that he gave his only begotten Son," we must know that the earth is the one place of greatest interest to all heaven. Not a sparrow can fall without notice.

Daniel's experience of contact with heaven is not an isolated one. A long series of such contacts started in the Garden of Eden and *has* continued and *will* continue till the new heaven and the new earth. They are all different because conditions differ, but all of them show how closely heaven is concerned with everything on the earth. For instance, Joshua was the leader of Israel in the conquest of the Promised Land. Before the fall of Jericho, the unseen captain of the Lord's hosts appeared to Joshua to reassure him:

> And it came to pass, when Joshua was by Jericho, that he lifted up his eyes and looked, and, behold, there stood a man over against him with his sword drawn in his hand; and Joshua went unto him, and said unto him, Art thou for us, or for our adversaries? And he said, Nay; but as captain of the host of the Lord am I now come.
>
> And Joshua fell on his face to the earth, and did worship, and said unto him, What saith my lord unto his servant? And the captain of the Lord's host said unto Joshua, Loose thy shoe from off thy foot; for the place whereon thou standest is holy. And Joshua did so.
>
> —Josh. 5: 13–15.

Thy [Daniel's] words were heard. Another time, too, "the Lord hearkened, and heard . . ., and a book of remembrance was written before him for them that feared the Lord, and that thought upon his name" (Mal. 3: 16).

During this dispensation, the Holy Spirit has been the means of contact between heaven and earth.

> Howbeit when he, the Spirit of truth, is come, he will guide you into all truth: for he shall not speak of himself; but whatsoever he shall hear,. that shall he speak: and he will shew you things to come. —John 16:13.

There are two special spiritual demonstrations, one at the beginning of the dispensation, the other at the end. These are so much alike that one prophecy in Joel will serve for both, although the last demonstration will be accompanied by more physical wonders. This prophecy was first spoken by Joel, then quoted and applied by Peter.

> And it shall come to pass afterward, that I will pour out my spirit upon all flesh; and your sons and your daughters shall prophesy, your old men shall dream dreams, your young men shall see visions: and also upon the servants and upon the handmaids in those days will I pour out my spirit.
>
> And I will shew wonders in the heavens and in the earth, blood, and fire, and pillars of smoke. The sun shall be turned into darkness, and the moon into blood, before the great and terrible day of the Lord come.
>
> And it shall come to pass, that whosoever shall call on the name of the Lord shall be delivered: for in mount Zion and in Jerusalem shall be deliverance, as the Lord hath said, and in the remnant whom the Lord shall call.
> —Joel 2:28–32.

The prince of the kingdom of Persia withstood me one and twenty days. The prince of the kingdom of Persia would be Satan's prince, not the earthly ruler. This gives us a look into Satan's realm, into the principalities and powers in heavenly places. Paul called Satan "the prince of the power of the air" (Eph. 2:2) *; Jesus called him "the prince of this

---

*Wherein in time past ye walked according to the course of this world, according to the prince of the power of the air, the spirit that now worketh in the children of disobedience. —Eph. 2:2.

world" (John 14:30).* Satan has an organized government, and the focal point seems also to be the earth. So important is the matter revealed in Chapter 11 that Satan made an all-out attempt to prevent its revelation. This vision is the unmasking of Satan in the last days. The fact that Satan was so concerned about it should give us an incentive to study it carefully.

A VISION OF THE LATTER DAYS

Now I am come to make thee understand what shall befall thy people in the latter days: for yet the vision is for many days. —Dan. 10:14.

The vision is for many days. This supports the Authorized Version rendering of verse 1: "The thing was true, but the time appointed was long." This was written 2500 years ago. Today, all the four great empires have come and gone. Now all the world is preparing for the final scenes as revealed to Daniel. These cluster around a man whom we call Antichrist.

What shall befall thy people. The term *thy people* may be taken broadly. Daniel's people are God's people. John the Baptist said, "Think not to say within yourselves, We have Abraham to our father: for I say unto you, that God is able of these stones to raise up children unto Abraham" (Matt. 3:9).

DANIEL NOT ALONE

Then said he, Knowest thou wherefore I come unto thee? and now will I return to fight with the prince of Per-

°Hereafter I will not talk much with you: for the prince of this world cometh, and hath nothing in me. —John 14:30.

sia: and when I am gone forth, lo, the prince of Grecia shall come. —Dan. 10:20.

Not only was heaven moved by things happening on the earth, but things on the earth were influenced by events in heaven. Satan's prince of Persia would be vanquished, and this vanquishing would insure the fall of Persia. But in place of the prince of Persia, Satan would put the prince of Greece, and Greece would rise to become a world power. All this happened on the earth, but the movement had its inception in heaven. Here is a basic truth that has been quite overlooked in this dispensation because it has not been in evidence in these days of the Spirit. For this reason, heaven again becoming a reality to the people of earth will come as a shock to the world.

The world's interest in outer space is going to take an unexpected turn when the heavenly silence is broken and the signs in the heavens begin to appear. Satan will break this silence first when he produces the man "whose coming is after the working of Satan." His coming is such a great event in prophecy that it is made the climax of all the visions given Daniel.

Daniel's first vision (ch. 2) ended with the kingdom of Christ; the second vision (ch. 7) ended with the same event but was preceded by the rise and fall of Antichrist. The third and fourth visions (ch. 8, 10–11) end with the downfall of Antichrist. The main purpose of three of the four visions is to reveal the rise, nature, exploits, and fall of Antichrist. To show the importance of this subject of Antichrist in the end time, compare the space given to it with the space given to other revelations.

Thus, as we approach the end, interest in Antichrist will build up. This man will dominate the scene from a few years before the Rapture until the battle of Armageddon at the coming of Christ.

THE SCRIPTURE OF TRUTH

But I will shew thee that which is noted in the scripture of truth: and there is none that holdeth with me in these things, but Michael your prince. —Dan. 10:21.

The scripture of truth. The earth is not the only place where records are kept. Malachi tells about some people who feared the Lord and "spake often one to another: and the Lord hearkened and heard it, and a book of remembrance was written before him for them that feared the Lord and that thought upon his name" (Mal. 3:16).

God is running a big business. We think of heaven as a primitive place of spirits roaming aimlessly. But heaven must be much farther advanced than the earth, where men build great industrial empires and invent marvelous machines for making, filing, and sorting all kinds of records. Imposing museums house the state papers of presidents. But man does nothing on earth that God has not done before. The world in which the spirits dwell is no less developed than the institutions of earth. Complete records are kept in heaven. Some day the books will be opened and men will be judged according to their works. The records will be on file. There is one difference: historical records are written in advance and kept under wraps.

There are secrets which even the angels do not share. Jesus mentioned things "kept secret from the foundation of the world." These secrets are kept primarily from Satan and apply particularly to the time of the Rapture. At the Rapture, Satan's "transfer" from heaven to earth is his first decisive defeat. The Rapture changes things in heaven as does no other event in prophecy.

Study 8

DANIEL'S FOURTH VISION
(Continued)

THE EXPLOITS OF ANTICHRIST
Daniel 11

THE EXPLOITS OF ANTICHRIST
Daniel 11

The rise of Antichrist will be Satan's preparation for the events at the Rapture. There will be changes in conditions on the earth that are hard to visualize and almost impossible to express. Daniel Chapter 11, therefore, contains much more than meets the eye and, like the parables of the kingdom, has a wealth of hidden truth that only the future will reveal. When the time actually comes, circumstances plus the operation of the Spirit will open these hidden things. The time is near. The first step is to understand the surface truth, but we should realize that that is only the beginning.

HELP FROM HEAVEN

Also I in the first year of Darius the Mede, even I [God's angel], stood to confirm and to strengthen him [Darius the Mede]. —Dan. 11:1.

Here, as in Daniel Chapter 10, we get a look behind the scenes. "There is a spiritual world unseen which is closely connected with the world of sense that meets our eyes. This chapter draws aside the veil and gives us a glimpse into the spirit world, where we see the hidden springs which govern the movements adverse to the people of God in our world, and also the counteracting agency of the loving

195

angels, who, by God's commission, defend His Church on earth." —Fausset.

The first year of Darius the Mede. This would be the first year of Persian control. Cyrus the Persian and Darius the Mede were joint rulers, for the empire was a union of the Medes and Persians. Darius seems to have been more a title than a name. A number of monarchs were called Darius.

I stood to confirm and to strengthen him (Darius the Mede). At that time Darius did not know God. Nor did he know that his success was due to the help of God's angel. God helped Darius' cause and he became one of the rulers of the world, not because of Darius, but because of Israel and Jerusalem. Now was the time for the captivity to end.

It is not without significance that the truth concerning the activities of heaven in the affairs of men should precede the revelations of this chapter. The opposition of Satan to this revelation also emphasizes its importance.

In the last days of the age probably the greatest shock to come to the people on the earth will be the realization that forces in the sky are planning to take over the earth. But it will be necessary for the people of God to understand what is happening. This knowledge will be a vital factor in the defeat of Satan. Here Satan's top secrets are revealed.

PERSIA AND GREECE

And now will I shew thee the truth. Behold, there shall stand up yet three kings in Persia; and the fourth shall be far richer than they all: and by his strength through his riches he shall stir up all against the realm of Grecia. And a mighty king shall stand up, that shall rule with great dominion, and do according to his will. And when he shall stand up, his kingdom shall be broken, and shall be divided toward the four winds of heaven; and not to his posterity, nor according to his dominion which he ruled: for his kingdom shall be plucked up, even for others beside those. —Dan. 11:2-4.

The prophecy of these two chapters starts at this point. In these few words we have the history of Persia and Greece. This had been covered in previous visions and was mentioned here to show the connection with what follows. Each successive vision supplements rather than duplicates the previous visions, so that specific details are added exactly where facts were lacking in other recitals. For instance, in the third vision we passed from the Grecian to the final empire of Antichrist without remark; now the gap will be filled in.

Persia had more than four rulers, but after the fourth, Xerxes, the empire declined. Xerxes' invasion of Greece was the beginning of the end of Persia because it raised up Alexander, who united Greece and began his conquest of the world. To avenge the wrongs done to Greece, Alexander invaded Persia in 334 B.C. Alexander was the first and last sole ruler of the Grecian empire. At his death his empire was divided into four parts over which Alexander's natural heirs did not rule. His generals took over.

FROM GREECE UNTIL THE RISE OF ROME

And the king of the south shall be strong, and one of his princes; and he shall be strong above him, and have dominion; his dominion shall be a great dominion.

And in those times there shall many stand up against the king of the south: also the robbers of thy people shall exalt themselves to establish the vision; but they shall fall.
—Dan. 11:5, 14.

Verses 5 to 14 trace the history of the fourth empire down to the rise of Rome. There was little of prophetic importance in these times between the Old and New Testaments. Nor do we have sufficient historical details to trace these prophecies with any more than guesses, though there seems to be some reference to the activities of Antiochus, who was the great persecutor of the Jews in Palestine.

THE ROMAN EMPIRE

So the king of the north shall come, and cast up a mount, and take the most fenced cities: and the arms of the south shall not withstand, neither his chosen people, neither shall there be any strength to withstand.

But he that cometh against him shall do according to his own will, and none shall stand before him: and he shall stand in the glorious land, which by his hand shall be consumed.

He shall also set his face to enter with the strength of his whole kingdom, and upright ones with him; thus shall he do: and he shall give him the daughter of woman, corrupting her: but she shall not stand on his side, neither be for him.

After this shall he turn his face unto the isles, and shall take many: but a prince for his own behalf shall cause the reproach offered by him to cease; without his own reproach he shall cause it to turn upon him. Then he shall turn his face toward the fort of his own land: but he shall stumble and fall, and not be found. —Dan. 11:15–19.

In these verses is briefly described the story of the rise and fall of the Roman Empire. Again, the purpose seems to be merely to complete the record, as it does not involve anything of prophetic importance as far as the last days are concerned. During this time the Church came into existence. In prophecy "a woman" represents a church. When the Roman power made the church a state church, it corrupted it, and it became the Roman Catholic Church.

THE RISE OF ANTICHRIST

Then shall stand up in his estate a raiser of taxes in the glory of the kingdom: but within few days he shall be destroyed, neither in anger, nor in battle. And in his estate shall stand up a vile person, to whom they shall not give the

honour of the kingdom: but he shall come in peaceably, and obtain the kingdom by flatteries. —Dan. 11:20, 21.

Then shall stand up in his estate—that is, as his successor. There was no successor to the Roman Empire. The kingdom was divided as Daniel said it would be, and this division was represented by the ten toes of the image. These nations, Daniel said, would exist till the kingdom of heaven be established. Thus the successor to the Roman Empire will not come till close to "the end," when for a short time the nations represented by the ten toes voluntarily join the empire of Antichrist. The new empire will be more of a restoration than a successor.

It is said that Antichrist takes three nations *by force.* This does not sound like a voluntary act, but it may be that these three were captive nations at the time and do not have the power of choice until they are restored to independence by Antichrist.

There is no question that this fourth vision ends with the battle of Armageddon and the destruction of Antichrist. The question is *When* does Antichrist appear? If we follow back from the end of the chapter to the place where the final man first appears, we have not one man, but two: (1) the raiser of taxes; (2) the vile person.

A raiser of taxes. When a man has the power to tax, he is in complete control of the empire. This raising of taxes may be a telling feature at the time of fulfillment; it concerns an element in the reign of Antichrist that makes him stand out as different from other dictators. Here is something to watch.

The "raiser of taxes" lasts only a short time before he is mysteriously killed. Revelation tells the same story but adds some details. He is "the little horn" of Daniel 7 and Daniel 8. He is also the seventh "head of the beast" in Revelation. When Satan is cast down to the earth, this head is "wounded to death," and then Satan brings him back to life. Here is Satan's way of acquiring a human body.

The little horn remains the same person but also becomes Satan in the flesh. This is a mystery. It is not explained, but is stated precisely. Revelation identifies the beast as the one who ascends out of the bottomless pit and goes into perdition—the lake of fire prepared for the devil and his angels (Rev. 17:8;* Matt. 25:41§).

> And there are seven kings [empires or rulers]: five are fallen [Assyria, Egypt, Babylon, Persia, Greece], and one is [Rome], and the other is not yet come [the little horn]; and when he cometh, he must continue a short space. —Rev. 17:10.

This corresponds exactly with Daniel. This mysterious person rises suddenly and restores world-empire by conquering three of the nations of the old empire (moving south, east, and toward Palestine). Then something happens to him. He is killed, Revelation says, by a sword wound, yet according to Daniel it is neither in anger nor in battle. This is as much as to say that it is a mysterious death for some sinister purpose. When Satan enters into him, he is at once the same man and a new man. This mystery is stated in so many words in Revelation: "And the beast that was, and is not, even he is the eighth, and is of the seven" (Rev. 17:11).

We have now the identity of "the raiser of taxes" of Daniel 11:20. This is the rise of the little horn.

In the glory of the kingdom. One translation of this phrase reads "to *the restoration of* the kingdom." The Roman Empire was the last of the world-empires, so that there will never be another world-empire except the restoration of the

---

* The beast that thou sawest was, and is not; and shall ascend out of the bottomless pit, and go into perdition: and they that dwell on the earth shall wonder, whose names were not written in the book of life from the foundation of the world, when they behold the beast that was, and is not, and yet is. —Rev. 17:8.

§ Then shall he say also unto them on the left hand, Depart from me, ye cursed, into everlasting fire, prepared for the devil and his angels. —Matt. 25:41.

empire under Antichrist. Even then, Antichrist's kingdom will be made up of about ten independent countries.

And in his estate shall stand up a vile person. Historians can find nothing in the past that could be a fulfillment of verses 20 and 21. The reason is simple: these details are still future. The symbol of the little horn applies to both the "raiser of taxes" and the "vile person," as one is a continuation of the other. But in this passage the two offices are distinguished. This is the entrance of Satan. From now on, we are dealing with the beast out of "the sea" (Rev. 13:1).*

To whom they shall not give the honour of the kingdom. To Satan, *not* receiving the honor of the kingdom is a definite identification and a humiliating one. Now we begin to see why Satan went to such lengths to prevent this defeat from being made known. This is war, and no general wants his strategy revealed or his movements published in advance; especially would he not want his defeat predicted. God reveals Satan's top secrets.

Satan will take over the kingdom, but will not be accorded the honor of a king. The position of dictator is the best he can attain. God gave dominion over the world to man. Men have a right to reign; Satan has no such right. The world will worship him as Satan because of his great power, but God's pronouncement will stand: man, not Satan, has dominion on the earth.

He shall come in peaceably. The previous vision said, "By peace he shall destroy many." Peace may be a very destructive force. The desire for peace in our time brought on World War II. Peace conferences may compromise with destructive forces and give them just the advantage needed to start a war. By means which are called peaceful, Russia has acquired control of a large part of the world. In nearly

---

* And I stood upon the sand of the sea, and saw a beast rise up out of the sea, having seven heads and ten horns, and upon his horns ten crowns, and upon his heads the name of blasphemy. —Rev. 13:1.

every case the desire for peace on the part of a smaller nation makes foreign penetration possible.

He shall . . . obtain the kingdom by flatteries. To obtain an empire by peace and flattery (or to use the modern term *intrigue*) is not new; but we have a new name for it—we call it cold war. This phrase expresses in ancient language what is now a very modern process.

ANTICHRIST CONSOLIDATES HIS POSITION

And with the arms of a flood shall they be overflown from before him, and shall be broken; yea, also the prince of the covenant. And after the league made with him he shall work deceitfully: for he shall come up, and shall become strong with a small people.

He shall enter peaceably even upon the fattest places of the province; and he shall do that which his fathers have not done, nor his fathers' fathers; he shall scatter among them the prey, and spoil, and riches: yea, and he shall forecast his devices against the strong holds, even for a time.
**　　　　　　　　　　　　　　　　　—Dan. 11:22–24.**

When all this happens, it will be understood perfectly. Yet these facts presuppose some conditions not yet in evidence. Therefore, it may help to look at the various versions of these verses. The Revised Version renders verse 22 as follows: "And the overwhelming forces shall be overwhelmed from before him, and shall be broken; yea, also the prince of the covenant."

Shall work deceitfully. *The Masoretic Text* translates verse 23 this way: "And after the league made with him he shall work deceitfully: and shall come up, and become strong with a little nation." *Young's Literal Translation* possibly gives the real sense: "And after they join themselves unto him [Antichrist], he worketh deceit, and hath increased, and hath been strong by a few of the nation." *The Vulgate* reads: "And after friendships with him, he shall work fraud, and shall go up and conquer with a small number." (The other versions make no substantial changes in verse 23.) Because these things have not yet happened and are future, those who try to put these events into the distant past are hard put to find anything of importance to which the words could apply.

In describing the rise of the little horn (Dan. 8), we are told that he "waxed exceeding great toward the south, and toward the east, and toward the pleasant land" (Dan. 8:9). His destination, then, will be Palestine. The changes that are now taking place and will take place make Palestine the prize of all world conquest. Palestine would even now be the center of world intrigue were it not for the fact that the Jews are there. Palestine's key position makes it "a must" for any world ruler. It will be number one on the list of nations to be conquered.

The question will arise: If Antichrist has so much power that he can easily put down the most formidable opposition (and the world worships him because of his ability to make war), and if Antichrist can almost control the world by this supernatural power, *how can he be stopped by so little a nation as Israel?* Why does he have to resort to chicanery and intrigue and "work deceitfully" (vs. 23)?

A harmony of all the prophecies would suggest a number of answers. First, there is the nation Israel itself. The return of the Jews, which will come before Antichrist's deceit, will be a *miraculous* event. There will be signs even more startling than those produced by Antichrist, and there will be evidence of God's protection for which even Antichrist will have respect. Until the way has been well prepared by some sharp practice by Antichrist, an outright invasion of Palestine cannot be even thought of.

In the second place, no small part of Antichrist's deceit will be the confirming of a covenant. This is to last seven years, but it will come to grief at the end of about 3½ years. The mention in verse 22 of "the prince of *the covenant*" would suggest that the Jews are the ones in view.

This covenant is sometimes rendered: "He shall make a *firm covenant*" (9:27). But this has little support, and does not make as much sense. The covenant is undoubtedly God's covenant with Israel concerning the land. It is this covenant that Antichrist confirms, thus trying to assume God's position as the protector of the Jews. Antichrist confirms the covenant "with many"—not with all the Jews, nor with Israel as a nation. How much the nation is involved is not said. The charge is not made that Israel as a nation officially accepts the overtures of Antichrist. The "many" may be leaders and men in power, but they alone are made responsible. The nation suffers for their disloyalty to God.

Young's Literal Translation is interesting here: "After they join themselves unto him, he worketh deceit, and hath increased, and hath been strong by a few of the nation." It is at this time that Antichrist will begin to negotiate with the Jews concerning Palestine, a process that will end disastrously for Israel. Daniel 9:26 concludes by saying, "*Unto the end of the war* desolations are determined." Young gives it more literally and more in harmony with the other versions: "Till the end is war." From the time that Antichrist confirms the covenant, there are wars.

Daniel expands this prophecy in Chapter 11. Desolations always follow wars. In the wars, Antichrist does not seem to have an undue advantage, and seems to be on about the same footing as the opposing nations. In his empire there will be open rebellion; in fact, after the Rapture there will be no peace. In Revelation, the second horseman takes peace from the earth. Jesus reviewed these times thus: "Nation shall rise against nation, and kingdom against kingdom" (Matt.

24:7). From the Rapture to the end, Antichrist's military power will steadily decline. After the final battle called Armageddon, the Jews will burn the weapons for firewood. How the weapons of war must have degenerated in that short space of time! To degenerate from atomic power and something like flying saucers, from intercontinental missiles and death-ray machines to weapons made by cutting branches out of trees, shows that something very drastic has happened.

This will not be because civilization has been destroyed and people have gone back to primitive life. Nothing like that will happen. Antichrist's original power is due to his contact with Satan, who at that time is a very powerful spirit with an untold number of angels. (He is "the prince of the power of the air.") His knowledge alone would enable him to outdo anything that man's limited knowledge could produce.

But at the Rapture, all that is changed. Satan will become a man, with many of man's limitations. It will still be true that Satan will be a spirit as well as a man. It will be a sort of incarnation, but the "dragon" will have lost his position and his angels and therefore much of his power.

On the other hand, the saints will have been caught up into heaven, from which vantage point, once occupied by Satan and his forces, relentless war will be waged on Satan. The seven last plagues, so fearfully described in Revelation, will be directed primarily against the kingdom of the beast. As a result, Satan's means of making destructive weapons will almost disappear from the earth.

So when the three spirits like frogs go forth to marshal the armies of the world, they will say, "Beat your plowshares into swords, and your pruninghooks into spears: let the weak say, I am strong." (Joel 3:10). Antichrist will become so weak militarily that he will not dare invade little Israel without all the armies of the world behind him. Even then, he will lose.

Through the whole of Daniel Chapter 11, we may follow
this decreasing in power and increasing in desperation.
Verse 44 of Daniel 11 says, "Tidings out of the east and
out of the north shall trouble him: therefore he shall go
forth with great fury to destroy, and utterly to make away
many." This is sheer desperation, a man at his wits' end.
Again we see why Satan did not want this story told.

**He shall do that which his fathers have not done, nor his
fathers' fathers.** His fathers are mentioned again in verse 37:
"Neither shall he regard the God of his fathers." The reference here is not to his own fathers and grandfathers. The
thought is not that Antichrist will be one in a line of conquerors. In this day of the atom, such a thing would be almost impossible. The word *fathers* is plural, meaning "those
who have gone before." Antichrist will do what his fathers
have not done—that is, what has not been done before.

Exactly what Antichrist does is not very clear, nor where
he does it. This will have to wait the event or the time close
enough to the event so that it may be anticipated. The
"province," mentioned in verse 24, may be Palestine, as that
is surely Antichrist's destination; but throughout the Old
Testament, the word *province* is used of any jurisdiction.

THE KING OF THE SOUTH

**And he shall stir up his power and his courage against
the king of the south with a great army; and the king of the
south shall be stirred up to battle with a very great and
mighty army; but he shall not stand: for they shall forecast
devices against him. —Dan. 11:25.**

The king of the south is usually taken to be Egypt;
however, Egypt was known to Daniel and is mentioned by
name even in this chapter. There would be no purpose in
making an enigma out of so simple a matter. The direction

must be taken in reference to Palestine. But king "of the south" does not mean that the country is itself south of Palestine. It could refer to any country that would naturally come into Palestine from the south. Historically, this has been Egypt. In other parts of this prophecy the "king of the south" probably refers to Egypt.

Concerning Egypt in the last days, there is a wealth of prophecy; in fact, Egypt is one of the most important countries in prophecy. From these we learn that Egypt will not be alone in her wars, for there will be a confederacy of nations, mostly all African, of which Egypt is only the leader. Thus, though "the king of the south" may include Egypt, more than Egypt is contained in this expression. It is also possible that Egypt will spread over a large part of North Africa. So great and powerful will Egypt become that her king will have visions of conquering the world. Jeremiah was amazed at what he saw concerning Egypt (Jer. 46:7–10).*

Miracle in the Sahara

The Sahara has opened up in astonishing ways. That neglected, barren area of the earth, that seemed good for nothing, has been proven to hold fabulous riches. European nations and others cast covetous eyes upon those vast deserts, and exploitation of the Sahara is gaining momentum daily. *Millions of tons of oil lie in the area of just one lot of oil derricks.* Just how much the Sahara holds is not known, but it may outshine all other petrol areas in the world. Diamonds have been discovered in the Tuareg areas, and

---

* Who is this that cometh up as a flood, whose waters are moved as the rivers? Egypt riseth up like a flood, and his waters are moved like the rivers; and he saith, I will go up, and will cover the earth; I will destroy the city and the inhabitants thereof. Come up, ye horses; and rage, ye chariots; and let the mighty men come forth; the Ethiopians and the Libyans, that handle the shield; and the Lydians, that handle and bend the bow.

For this is the day of the Lord God of hosts, a day of vengeance, that he may avenge him of his adversaries: and the sword shall devour, and it shall be satiate and made drunk with their blood: for the Lord God of hosts hath a sacrifice in the north country by the river Euphrates. —Jer. 46:7–10.

also platinum. To lay hold of the "black gold" and other riches, the nations pour in money and men, with no thought of the cost.

The first prophet to call attention to this remarkable change in the desert was Isaiah. He may have had more than the Sahara in mind, and may have been talking about deserts in general. But when these things begin to happen in the greatest and most barren desert of the earth, it is time we took the prophecy into consideration.

> The wilderness and the solitary place [dry land] shall be glad for them; and the desert shall rejoice, and blossom as the rose. It shall blossom abundantly, and rejoice even with joy and singing: the glory of Lebanon shall be given unto it, the excellency of Carmel and Sharon, they shall see the glory of the Lord, the excellency of our God.
> —Isa. 35:1, 2.

What is happening in the Sahara would be headline news were it not for the fact that so many things are happening in other parts of the world. One of the most sensational developments in the history of the world is taking place almost without notice. The first important discovery in the Sahara was water. There is enough water underground to transform the Sahara Desert into one vast garden and to make it "blossom as the rose." The only thing required to produce this water would be power to bring it up out of the ground.

That brings us to the next important discovery concerning the Sahara. There is also oil there, not just a little oil here and there but vast quantities, possibly even greater er than the oil reserves of the United States. Only the Middle East has more oil than the Sahara. This oil is of such a high grade that, without refining, it can be used to power the engines necessary to bring the water out of the ground. So not only water is in the Sahara, but the power is there to produce the water. This oil now belongs to France, and if France could solve her African problems, she could become the richest nation of Europe.

But the picture has another side. All Europe runs on oil—its automobiles, its factories, and many of its furnaces. All the Arab states of the Middle East owe their prosperity, if not their existence, to the royalties from oil. If France or any other country could replace those Arab countries as the supplier of oil to the world, it might ruin financially all of those Arab lands.

Egypt is trying to get a corner on oil. It now controls the Suez Canal by which a large part of the oil reaches Europe. It tried, by a union with Syria, to get control of the pipeline that pipes the oil to the Mediterranean Sea. Oil is the biggest single factor in the development of the Middle East.

If France or the U.S. should start producing oil on a large scale in the Sahara, Egypt's whole program would be threatened. But the Arabs are trying to control the entire northern coast of Africa across which the pipelines would have to go to reach the sea. So, a contest for North Africa is a contest for the control of the whole world.

France was wise enough not to try to exploit the Sahara oil herself. That would take too long and be too costly. Instead, France offered a fifty per cent interest in the oil of the Sahara to any American or other big oil company that would go in there and take the oil out. Nearly every big oil company in the United States has responded and is now rushing all kinds of machinery and equipment into the Sahara. The map shows the places where these companies now operate and the pipelines that are being contemplated to take the oil to the Sea.

Inasmuch as the emergence of France as a great oil-producing state would completely upset the plans of the Communists for world domination, you may expect that the Russians will put on an all-out contest to keep this from happening. As long as one-half of the world's oil supplies are in the hands of the Arabs, it is possible for the Com-

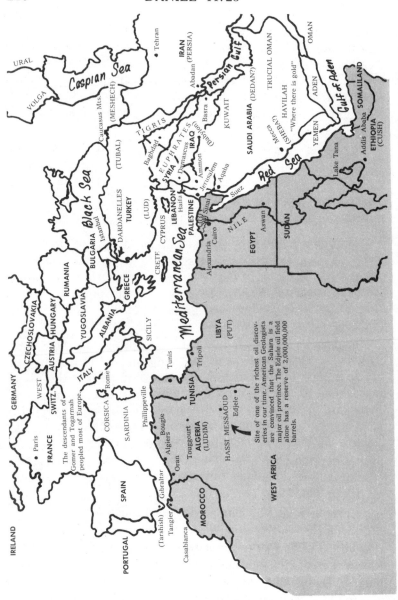

munists to be a continual threat to the world. But if all the oil used by the world should be in the hands of the western powers, the Communists would lose their greatest leverage for power. Therefore the political crisis in France is not merely a local affair but is a part of the world-wide contest for power.

In this contest for power, Egypt is the key country and may emerge as one of the greatest countries in the world. The Communists will certainly help Egypt get control of Africa. Jeremiah saw this revival of Egypt as coming in the last days. He even expressed his surprise that a country as weak as Egypt should suddenly become a world power. Jeremiah said,

> Who is this that riseth up like the Nile, whose waters toss themselves like the rivers? Egypt riseth up like the Nile, and his waters toss themselves like the rivers: and he saith, I will rise up, I will cover the earth; I will destroy cities and the inhabitants thereof.
> Go up, ye horses; and rage, ye chariots; and let the mighty men go forth: Cush and Put, that handle the shield; and the Ludim, that handle and bend the bow.
> —Jer. 46:7–9, R.V.

In the same passage Jeremiah lists the countries that will be confederate with Egypt, possibly not at the start but before the day of the Lord. These countries could include all of North Africa from the Red Sea to the Atlantic Ocean. Ethiopia (Cush) and Libya (Put) would reach half way across the continent of Africa. There have been two places known as Lydia or Lud: one was Turkey and the other was North Africa, west of Libya. Most commentators seem to think that it is the African Lydia rather than the Asiatic Lydia that is meant here by Jeremiah. If that is the case, it means that Jeremiah predicted the expansion of Egypt across North Africa. Thus Egypt would control all the oil of Africa as well as that of the Middle East. This will be an interesting prophecy to watch develop.

AN IMPORTANT CONFERENCE

In Africa things are changing very fast. The whole continent is rich. With proper leadership, Africa could become the greatest force in the world, actually rivaling that of Antichrist. Daniel suggests as much:

Yea, they that feed of the portion of his meat shall destroy him, and his army shall overflow: and many shall fall down slain. And both these kings' hearts shall be to do mischief, and they shall speak lies at one table; but it shall not prosper: for yet the end shall be at the time appointed.
—Dan. 11:26, 27.

Both these kings ... shall speak lies at one table. The only kings in view here are "the king of the south" and Antichrist. The conference ("speaking ... at one table") will be a famous one at which agreements will be made, but neither king will have any intention of keeping them. This war will be won apparently by Antichrist. The "king of the south" will be given a set back, but is not destroyed and will try again.

Yet the end shall be at the time appointed. When these things happen, we are approaching the final defeat of Satan which marks "the end." This expression "at the time appointed" marks either the end of one phase or the beginning of a new one. Many things will be happening which cannot all be told in chronological sequence.

Isaiah, Jeremiah, and Ezekiel all have much to say about the very nations which make up the territory of "the king of the south," "the king of the north," and Antichrist. At first sight there seems little in common. Revelation deals extensively with the same time, yet does not mention most of the movements of Antichrist recorded in Daniel. Revelation is interested in these events only to the extent that they concern the Church or the saints. Isaiah, Jeremiah, and Ezekiel make a point of telling what God will do to these countries because of their treatment of the Jews. Only Daniel traces the exploits of Antichrist as such, regardless of whether they involve the nations, or the saints, or the Jews.

ANTICHRIST TURNS HIS ATTENTION TO ISRAEL

Then shall he [Antichrist] return into his land with great riches; and his heart shall be against the holy covenant; and he shall do exploits, and return to his own land. —Dan. 11:28.

Antichrist's struggle with "the king of the south" will have the immediate effect of turning him back so that he will not be able at that time to continue his campaign against Israel. He still will not have the one essential to world power—the World Island—Palestine.

The campaign against "the king of the south" will be successful and richly profitable. Many side-wars and excursions into other countries along the way will add to Antichrist's riches, but the main objective is still unattainable. He will brood over the holy covenant which is recorded in Genesis 17:3–8.

And Abram fell on his face: and God talked with him, saying, As for me, behold, my covenant is with thee, and thou shalt be a father of many nations. Neither shall thy name any more be called Abram, but thy name shall be Abraham; for a father of many nations have I made thee.

And I will make thee exceedingly fruitful, and I will make nations of thee, and kings shall come out of thee. And I will establish my covenant between me and thee and thy seed after thee in their generations for an everlasting covenant, to be a God unto thee, and to thy seed after thee.

And I will give unto thee, and to thy seed after thee, the land wherein thou art a stranger, all the land of Canaan, for an everlasting possession; and I will be their God. —Gen. 17:3–8.

Abraham's first impression of Palestine must have been a discouraging one, for there was a famine in the land, and Abraham had to move on into Egypt to find pasture for his animals. But at the time of Israel's exodus from Egypt, the land of Palestine was said to be "flowing with milk and honey." Then from the Exodus till the final dispersion, Palestine seems again to have been no better than many other lands. Nevertheless God called it a land that He had espied for them, "the glory of all lands" (Ezek. 20:6).

For nearly 2,000 years Palestine has been a barren land and is still barren, except for the portions that the Jews have laboriously reclaimed. It has some natural resources, but its great value is its position at the crossroads of the world. As long as Africa was a dark continent, China asleep, and Russia behind an iron curtain, Israel's central position was of only slight advantage.

But now, Africa is vibrating with energy and ready to take its place among the world's great; now China and all the East are becoming of age; now Russia cannot remain an isolated country forever. All this affects the future of Palestine, for all the immense commerce and trade from three continents would naturally pass through Palestine. It has harbors on both the Mediterranean and South Seas; it is the natural capital of the world. Some day it *will be* the capital of the world.

> And it shall come to pass in the last days, that the mountain of the Lord's house shall be established in the top of the mountains, and shall be exalted above the hills; and all nations shall flow unto it.
>
> And many people shall go and say, Come ye, and let us go up to the mountain of the Lord, to the house of the God of Jacob; and he will teach us of his ways, and we will walk in his paths; for out of Zion shall go forth the law, and the word of the Lord from Jerusalem.
>
> —Isa. 2:2, 3.

His [Antichrist's] heart shall be against the holy covenant. The seal of the covenant was the ark, often called "the ark of the covenant." The ark went before the Israelites into battle and assured them of victory. The first victory, the fall of Jericho, was the token of the Israelites' possession of the whole land. By the power signified by the ark, they were supposed to take all the land. Palestine was the *promised* land, and the ark was the outward symbol of the promise or covenant. It was the only thing in the tabernacle that looked forward to the Second Coming of Christ and the final and complete possession of the land by the Jews.

If at this point we could trace, through history and prophecy, the story of this covenant and the ark which guaranteed it, we would realize what an effect the reappearance of the ark in the last days would have both on the Jews and on Antichrist. When Antichrist wants above all else the land of Palestine, the greatest deterrent to his ambitions is the holy covenant. No wonder his heart is "*against* the holy covenant."

Everything that happens from now on must be viewed in this light. The nations want Palestine. The Jews are there, but they are defenseless except for the covenant; so Antichrist must find some way of nullifying the holy covenant. It has been done before, for Balac accomplished it by the "doctrine of Balaam, who taught Balac to cast a stumblingblock before the children of Israel, to eat things sacrificed unto idols, and to commit fornication" (Rev. 2:14). This process is known today as infiltration. It is Satan's oldest trick, sometimes expressed in these words: "If you can't fight it, join it." This has always been the policy of modernists when confronted with an evangelistic back-to-the-Bible movement. If they can, they fight it. If it is too big to fight, they embrace it and eventually control it.

This is Satan's covenant and he offers to become its protector. Such has been Satan's successful strategy throughout the ages. For emphasis it should be repeated that the nation of Israel is never charged with making this treasonable deal with Antichrist. Daniel says that Antichrist "shall confirm the covenant with many," that is, with many of those in power (Dan. 9:27), though the actual number as compared with all Israel would be few. Here, then, we are told, that Antichrist becomes strong with a few people or with a few of the nation.

JACOB'S TROUBLE

At the time appointed he [Antichrist] shall return, and come toward the south; but it shall not be as the former, or as the latter. For the ships of Chittim shall come against him: therefore he shall be grieved, and return, and have indignation against the holy covenant; so shall he do; he shall even return, and have intelligence with them that forsake the holy covenant.

And arms shall stand on his part, and they shall pollute the sanctuary of strength, and shall take away the daily sacrifice, and they shall place the abomination that maketh desolate. And such as do wickedly against the covenant shall he corrupt by flatteries: but the people that do know their God shall be strong, and do exploits. —Dan. 11:29-32.

At the time appointed begins a new subject. In this instance, the subject matter is well developed in prophecy and goes by many names. Jeremiah calls it "Jacob's trouble."

For, lo, the days come, saith the Lord, that I will bring again the captivity of my people Israel and Judah, saith the Lord: and I will cause them to return to the land that I gave to their fathers, and they shall possess it.

And these are the words that the Lord spake concerning Israel and concerning Judah. For thus saith the Lord; We have heard a voice of trembling, of fear, and not of peace. Ask ye now, and see whether a man doth travail with child? wherefore do I see every man with his hands on his loins, as a woman in travail, and all faces are turned into paleness?

> Alas! for that day is great, so that none is like it: it is even *the time of Jacob's trouble;* but he shall be saved out of it.
>
> For it shall come to pass in that day, saith the Lord of hosts, that I will break his yoke from off thy neck, and will burst thy bonds, and strangers shall no more serve themselves of him: But they shall serve the Lord their God, and David their king, whom I will raise up unto them. —Jer. 30:3–9.

The time is known: it is the last half of Daniel's 70th week. Revelation identifies it as follows:

> But the court which is without the temple leave out, and measure it not; for it is given unto the Gentiles: and the holy city shall they tread under foot forty and two months. —Rev. 11:2.

Jesus called it "the times of the Gentiles":

> And when ye shall see Jerusalem compassed with armies, then know that the desolation thereof is nigh.
>
> Then let them which are in Judæa flee to the mountains; and let them which are in the midst of it depart out; and let not them that are in the countries enter thereinto. For these be the days of vengeance, that all things which are written may be fulfilled.
>
> But woe unto them that are with child, and to them that give suck, in those days! for there shall be great distress in the land, and wrath upon this people. And they shall fall by the edge of the sword, and shall be led away captive into all nations: and Jerusalem shall be trodden down of the Gentiles, until *the times of the Gentiles* be fulfilled. —Luke 21:20–24.

There is so much prophecy concerning this brief period of time that a thorough exposition would amount to a review of the entire prophetic Scriptures. Probably the most complete single view is found in Ezekiel 38 and 39, which deal with this invasion of Palestine and its results in reference to the future of Israel.

For the ships of Chittim shall come against him (Antichrist). This seems to be Antichrist's third attempt. The first and the second will achieve many successes but will fail in the vital point of acquiring control of Israel. This third time a new enemy, Chittim, will threaten him. Those who try to find some historic event to which this passage might apply make the ships of Chittim to be the ships of Rome. But it is highly improbable that Antichrist's own ships should come against him. Sometimes the name Chittim is applied to Cyprus. Yet it is more likely used to denote a country which was unknown in Daniel's day but which will arise in time to trouble Antichrist and to cause him to panic. Thus in the end we will see Antichrist acting in desperation, throwing all caution to the winds.

And arms shall stand on his part. "This word *arms* is not to be understood as weapons (a misunderstanding possible in English). *Arms* here stands as a symbol of physical strength generally."—*Pulpit Commentary.* "Arms shall stand on his part" could be translated, *"he shall set physical forces in motion."* The nations cannot prevent infiltration of Palestine by the consent of the Jewish officials; nevertheless, actual physical occupancy would certainly bring about a world crisis. Again, this whole story is told by Ezekiel (Chapters 38 and 39).

They shall place the abomination that maketh desolate. This abomination of desolation has been mentioned before (8:13; 9:27; see also 12:11). The actual abomination is not described in Scripture, unless we apply to it the statement of Paul:

> Let no man deceive you by any means: for that day shall not come, except there come a falling away first, and that man of sin be revealed, the son of perdition; who opposeth and exalteth himself above all that is called God, or that is worshipped; so that *he as God sitteth in the temple of God, shewing himself that he is God.* —II Thess. 2:3, 4.

But the people that do know their God shall be strong and do exploits. Although the word *exploits* is not in the Hebrew, the word expresses the meaning. There will be resistance to Antichrist, in fact, very effective resistance. We do not have the full story in any one place, for so many things will be happening at once that a consecutive narration is well nigh impossible. There will be activity among the nations—the greatest war of all time is brewing. There will also be activity in heaven—trumpets are blown, vials are poured out. There will be activity in the world of evil spirits which will overrun the earth. There will be activity of an evangelistic nature. This will be led by two witnesses from heaven. At the end of this "woe" we are told, "The same hour was there a great earthquake, and the tenth part of the city fell, and in the earthquake were slain of men seven thousand; and the remnant were affrighted, and gave glory to the God of heaven" (Rev. 11: 13). This earthquake will be the only one of the seven last plagues that will cause anyone to give glory to God, and something will be added to this one. Malachi suggests what this will be:

> Behold, I will send you Elijah the prophet before the coming of the great and dreadful day of the Lord: and he shall turn the heart of the fathers to the children, and the heart of the children to their fathers, lest I come and smite the earth with a curse. —Mal. 4: 5, 6.

Probably much more will be happening in those closing days than can be recorded. We have only a little information, sometimes not enough in any one place to make a harmony possible.

WITNESSING UNDER ANTICHRIST

And they that understand among the people shall instruct many: yet they shall fall by the sword, and by flame, by captivity, and by spoil, many days. Now when they shall fall, they shall be holpen with a little help: but many shall cleave to them with flatteries. And some of them of understanding shall fall, to try them, and to purge, and to make

them white, even to the time of the end: because it is yet for a time appointed. —Dan. 11:33–35.

They that understand among the people shall instruct many. We find here the purpose of this prophecy. Its greatest value will be in times of trouble. Satan's persecutions will have little effect on those who understand what is happening and know how God is working out His plan. When the world will suddenly be plunged into distress, when "the lights go out" again all over the world, and when the end of humanity will seem near, it will be those who know the prophecy who will keep the Church together and who will even advance the Kingdom. The prophetic Word will be for the time of the end; it is designed for the end; it is preserved for the end; and it will be made known "at the appointed time."

Yet they shall fall by the sword, and by flame, by captivity, and by spoil. These verses furnish a contact with other prophecies. They may be taken as a summary. They cover "many days" and tell what will be happening in the field of evangelism during the whole time from the Rapture to the coming of Christ. There will not be a time when God will not have His people on the earth. As long as there are witnesses, there will be witnessing.

Many days. The word *many* is not in the original. The Peshitta reads, "a thousand days." This is a relatively brief time. If it coincides with the testimony of the two witnesses, the time will be 3½ years. It ends, according to Jesus, with His return.

The Peshitta renders verse 33 as follows: "The dispersed of the people shall instruct many, and they shall fall by the sword, and by fire, by captivity, and by spoil, *a thousand days.*" In the Authorized Version the actual number of days of trouble is in italics; that is, it is left indefinite. But it is figured in days, not years. These troubles could last a few years, but not enough to be termed many years.

Immediately after the Rapture, there will be a time called "the tribulation, the great one," out of which will come the tribulation saints. Their experience will be very close to that described in verses 33 to 35. Apparently there will be two groups of people—many will be killed, but others will be sealed as a protection from the plagues. Whether or not these two groups include all the saved at the time, Revelation does not say. According to other Scriptures, there may be some in prison and in hiding not included in either group.*

How much witnessing, if any, will be done by the 144,000 is not said. As far as Revelation is concerned, the 144,000 will remain on Mount Zion, where there will be safety. It is certain they will not be able to leave Palestine; but we know that throughout Palestine there will be effective preaching even under persecution, for captive saints will be taken before kings. The fact that they appear before kings shows the effectiveness of their testimony.

Although the gospel is to be preached in all the world so that people will be saved from every kindred, tongue, and nation, according to Revelation 14:6 this preaching seems to be done from heaven. After the Rapture heaven is where the preachers will be:

> I saw another angel fly in the midst of heaven, having the everlasting gospel to preach unto them that dwell on the earth, and to every nation, and kindred, and tongue, and people.

Revelation 6:9–11 says that the Church will undergo severe persecution and most, if not all, of its believing members will be martyrs.

> When he had opened the fifth seal, I saw under the altar the souls of them that were slain for the word of God, and for the testimony which they held: and they cried with a loud voice, saying, How long, O Lord, holy and true, dost thou not judge and avenge our blood on them that dwell on the earth?

* This is developed more fully in **The Olivet Discourse.**

> And white robes were given unto every one of them; and it was said unto them, that they should rest yet for a little season, until their fellowservants also and their brethren, that should be killed as they were, should be fulfilled.

There is no record of these Christians doing exploits, although in those days of unusual things, doing exploits cannot be ruled out. In any case, their doing exploits will not save their lives. On the other hand, in Israel there will be a powerful testimony. At the beginning, Israel will be comparatively free from interference by Antichrist. It is possible that the Jews themselves would persecute Christian preachers. Jesus gave us a very complete fill-in on this situation on the occasion of His sending out the twelve disciples. Though He gave them instructions as to their conduct on the trip, yet His mind was far away, for He was thinking, as usual, about the time of the end when other missionaries would take the message of the kingdom over the hills and plains of Palestine. Soon He forgot about the immediate journey and began giving instructions to those who would go forth just before His coming again. He said:

> Behold, I send you forth as sheep in the midst of wolves: be ye therefore wise as serpents, and harmless as doves. But beware of men: for they will deliver you up to the councils, and they will scourge you in their synagogues; and ye shall be *brought before governors and kings for my sake, for a testimony* against them and the Gentiles.
>
> But when they deliver you up, take no thought how or what ye shall speak: for it shall be given you in that same hour what ye shall speak. For it is not ye that speak, but the Spirit of your Father which speaketh in you. And the brother shall deliver up the brother to death, and the father the child: and the children shall rise up against their parents, and cause them to be put to death.
>
> And ye shall be hated of all men for my name's sake: but he that endureth to the end shall be saved. But

when they persecute you in this city, flee ye into another:
for verily I say unto you, Ye shall not have gone over
the cities of Israel, till the Son of man be come.
                                        —Matt. 10:16–23.

If the preachers are to go only to the people of Israel,
how is it that they must appear before kings? Jesus also answered this question, when He said:

They shall fall by the edge of the sword, and shall
be *led away captive* into all nations: and Jerusalem shall
be trodden down of the Gentiles, until the times of the
Gentiles be fulfilled. —Luke 21:24.

If the preachers are led away captive into all nations, they
may well stand before kings. But why should kings be interested in them? It is because, as Daniel says, the Christians do
exploits. Jesus also told what these exploits are:

And when he had called unto him his twelve
disciples, he gave them *power* against unclean spirits,
to cast them out, and *to heal* all manner of sickness and
all manner of disease. —Matt. 10:1.

And these signs shall follow them that believe; In
my name shall they *cast out devils;* they shall *speak with
new tongues;* they shall *take up serpents;* and if they
drink any deadly thing, it shall not hurt them; they shall
lay hands on the sick, and they shall recover.

So then after the Lord had spoken unto them, he
was received up into heaven, and sat on the right hand
of God. And they went forth, and preached every where,
*the Lord working with them, and confirming the word
with signs following.* —Mark 16:17–20.

**Even to the time of the end, because it is yet for a time
appointed.** This reference to the end time—to the very end
of the reign of Antichrist—brings to a close this portion of
the prophecy, and thus follows the prophetic method of dealing with only one line of thought at a time. Now we will, in
effect, retrace our steps as to time and take up another line
of thought concerning the nature and movements of Antichrist during the closing days.

ANTICHRIST EXALTS HIMSELF

And the king shall do according to his will; and he shall exalt himself, and magnify himself above every god, and shall speak marvelous things against the God of gods, and shall prosper till the indignation be accomplished: for that that is determined shall be done. —Dan. 11:36.

This briefly summarizes the religious side of Antichrist's reign. He will exalt himself above all other gods and will speak great words against the Most High. It is important to understand Satan's attitude toward God. The false gods he handles with ease; he merely exalts his throne above them. But when it comes to the true God, Satan will be embarrassed. He can not exalt himself that high; he cannot silence the martyrs; he cannot touch the two witnesses. He can, as Paul says, sit in the temple of God showing himself that he is God, but he cannot make his claim stick. He will have to resort to speaking bold words against God. In doing this, he will unwittingly acknowledge God.

Notice that Antichrist is *not* "like" Christ. He does not claim to be Christ; he claims to be *a god* and is very much against the true God. He is Antichrist only in the sense that he is *against* Christ.

THE GOD OF HIS FATHERS

Neither shall he regard the God of his fathers, nor the desire of women, nor regard any god: for he shall magnify himself above all. But in his estate shall he honour the God of forces: and a god whom his fathers knew not shall he honour with gold, and silver, and with precious stones, and pleasant things. —Dan. 11:37, 38.

These verses are sometimes quoted to support the erroneous theory that Antichrist will be a Jew. Actually, he will hate the Jews and try to wipe them off the earth. In the end he will come against them in the battle of Armageddon. There is not the slightest evidence anywhere in Scripture that Antichrist will be a Jew or a false Messiah.

Neither shall he regard the God of his fathers. It does not say "the" fathers but "his" fathers. A Gentile can have fathers or ancestors. "His fathers" is mentioned also in verse 24: "He shall do that which his fathers have not done nor his fathers' fathers." This reference could not possibly be to the Israelitish fathers, but simply means that Antichrist will have no regard for the God worshipped by his ancestors. Instead, he will set himself up as a new God.

Nor the desire of women. This is sometimes said to mean the desire of Jewish women to be the mother of Messiah. But Jewish women in general have no such desire or any knowledge of any such possibility; and even if they did, it would have nothing to do with the exaltation of Antichrist. His interest in himself is so great that he has no time nor thought for women.

In his estate shall he honour the God of forces. Antichrist will regard the "god of forces," a strange god whom he will set up. He is interested only in gaining power and control of the world.

A STRANGE GOD

Thus shall he do in the most strong holds with a strange god, whom he shall acknowledge and increase with glory: and he shall cause them to rule over many, and shall divide the land for gain. —Dan. 11:39.

There are so many different renderings of this verse that the real meaning is hard to determine. It seems to be a summary of all that is past, in preparation for the final scenes that are to follow. The reference to a strange god will be understood only when we are near enough to the event for such a god to appear.

"THE TIME OF THE END"

And at the time of the end shall the king of the south push at him: and the king of the north shall come against him like a whirlwind, with chariots, and with horsemen, and with many ships; and he shall enter into the countries, and shall overflow and pass over. —Dan. 11:40.

At the time of the end. Here we have arrived at the time that has been the announced goal throughout this chapter. A number of prophets tell (sometimes in great detail) of the final invasion of Israel and the battle around Jerusalem, somewhat ambiguously called the battle of Armageddon. "The end" *never* means the end of the world, but the goal of all prophecy—the defeat of Satan and the coming of the kingdom of God.

The king of the south shall push at him. The king of the south has always been thought of as Egypt—he is called Egypt in the Septuagint. The "king of the south" would not have to be the same person or country throughout history, and he could be any king coming in from the south. Our need is only to determine who this king is at the time of the fulfillment of this prophecy. The practice of the prophets was to call known countries by name and to use some other means to identify unknown countries, or countries that would later come into existence.

We are dealing now with the very end. Great changes will be coming, especially in Africa and other backward countries. Before and during the reign of Antichrist, many new and powerful nations will undoubtedly arise. In that day the king of the south could represent some nation or nations not now in view, or it could represent a new combination of nations. It is quite certain that Egypt alone is not meant because in verse 42 Egypt is mentioned by name as a nation entirely apart from the king of the south. This would not rule out the possibility that Egypt could be a part of the group of nations whose head would be known as "the king of the south."

And the king of the north shall come against him [Antichrist] like a whirlwind. Here is another unknown country. The king of the north is not Antichrist. He will come against Antichrist. Again, we must think of Palestine as being the place from which directions are considered. North and south do not necessarily refer to countries lying exactly north or south of Palestine but to countries that would naturally enter Palestine from those directions.

Nebuchadnezzar, king of Babylon, is spoken of as coming from the north (Ezek. 26:7).* The actual identity of this king of the north may not be known until the time approaches and we can see how the nations are lining up. According to Ezekiel there will be a new Babylonian Empire of great power and extent which will destroy Egypt (Ezek. 26-28). Such a power would be a threat to Antichrist. After the Rapture the kingdom of the beast is never peaceful. Unto the very end, wars are determined.

This raises an interesting question: What will happen to Antichrist's supernatural weapons by which at first he conquered everything in sight? We seem in the passage to have reverted to old-fashioned weapons and tools of war. It will be manpower against manpower until, in the final battle, the whole manpower of the world will be mobilized. There are places in Scripture where bombs and atomic power are suggested by the description, but they are rare. The tendency is toward primitive weapons, even weapons of wood. After the final defeat of Antichrist and the nations that come

* For thus saith the Lord God; Behold, I will bring upon Tyrus Nebuchadrezzar king of Babylon, a king of kings, from the north, with horses, and with chariots, and with horsemen, and companies, and much people. —Ezek. 26:7.

against Jerusalem, the people that are left will burn the weapons of firewood for seven years (Ezek. 39:9, 10).* These weapons will be handmade:

> Proclaim ye this among the Gentiles; Prepare war, wake up the mighty men, let all the men of war draw near; let them come up: Beat *your plowshares into swords, and your pruninghooks into spears:* let the weak say, I am strong.
> Assemble yourselves, and come, all ye heathen, and gather yourselves together round about: thither cause thy mighty ones to come down, O Lord. —Joel 3:9–11.

This will be a far cry from jets and missiles, death rays and gas. What will have happened? Several things. *First*: Before the Rapture Satan's power will stem from his position in the heavens, for he is the prince of the power of the air. But when Satan is cast out of heaven down to the earth, this advantage will be lost.

Second: The plagues, sent from heaven and detailed in Revelation, will be directed at Antichrist and his kingdom. The plagues will be controlled and intelligently applied by heavenly agents. Their purpose will be to destroy the results of sin; and so, the factories for the manufacture of weapons will naturally not be overlooked. So thorough will be the work of the angels with the trumpets and vials that for the battle of Armageddon, the armies will have to depend on weapons hastily constructed of wood.

EDOM, MOAB, EGYPT

He shall enter also into the glorious land, and many countries shall be overthrown: but these shall escape out of his hand, even Edom, and Moab, and the chief of the

---

* And they that dwell in the cities of Israel shall go forth, and shall set on fire and burn the weapons, both the shields and the bucklers, the bows and the arrows, and the handstaves, and the spears, and they shall burn them with fire seven years: so that they shall take no wood out of the field, neither cut down any out of the forests; for they shall burn the weapons with fire: and they shall spoil those that spoiled them, and rob those that robbed them, saith the Lord God. —Ezek. 39:9, 10.

**children of Ammon. He shall stretch forth his hand also upon
the countries: and the land of Egypt shall not escape.**

   **But he shall have power over the treasures of gold and
of silver, and over all the precious things of Egypt: and the
Libyans and the Ethiopians shall be at his steps.**

—Dan. 11:41-43.

From the beginning of the invasion of Palestine until
the coming of the Lord, 3½ years will elapse. At the very
end, all nations will be gathered together and will enter
Palestine from two directions, north and east. Usually armies
marching from the east followed the Euphrates River, and
this brought them into Palestine from the northeast.
Countries southeast of Palestine would not be in the line of
march and so would escape. Edom and Moab are not countries now, but great changes are in store for the Middle

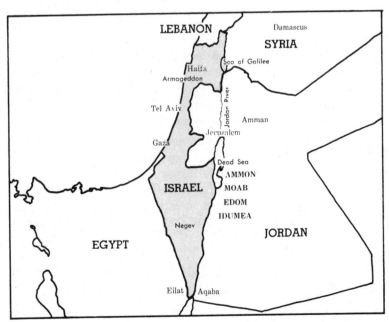

East. Ammon could be identified as Jordan, but even that may change.

It is strange that Edom and Moab should be mentioned here. They lie south and east of Israel and are among the places that will be severely punished for their treatment of the Jews. It is understandable why they should escape Antichrist; he will enter from the north and will be destroyed before he reaches that far south.

The Lord will come from the east (see Matt. 24:27).* Other places––all of them in the same general location––which are mentioned in connection with the return of Christ are Teman, Mt. Paran (Hab. 3:3)§ and Bozrah (Isa. 63:1).¶ Edom is mentioned there also. When Christ first appears, it will be from that direction; so, as He appears over the horizon, He will seem to come from those countries. Other prophecies indicate that, although these countries escape the pressure of Antichrist, they will not escape the judgments of God (Isa. 34; Ezek. 25:8–14).

The land of Egypt shall not escape. Here there are a variety of translations. The meaning seems to be that Egypt will not be a *place of escape*. One ancient version reads, "And he shall stretch his hand upon the land and the land of Egypt *shall not be for salvation.*"

Whenever Palestine was threatened with war, there was always the tendency to look to Egypt for help or for a place of escape. Abraham went into Egypt to wait out the famine; the sons of Jacob went to Egypt to buy food; Egypt was a place of refuge for many Jews, including Jeremiah at the time of the Captivity; the parents of Jesus took Him to Egypt to escape Herod.

---

* For as the lightning cometh out of the east, and shineth even unto the west; so shall also the coming of the Son of man be. —Matt. 24:27.

§ God came from Teman, and the Holy One from mount Paran. Selah. His glory covered the heavens, and the earth was full of his praise. —Hab. 3:3.

¶ Who is this that cometh from Edom, with dyed garments from Bozrah? this that is glorious in his apparel, travelling in the greatness of his strength? I that speak in righteousness, mighty to save. —Isa. 63:1.

But in the end time, there will be no escape to Egypt; in fact, there will be no Egypt. Egypt will yet have a big place in the process of the return of the Jews. The time will come when a large part of the Jewish population of the world will be banished to Egypt (Deut. 28:68).* There will be so many Jews in Egypt that five cities will speak Hebrew (Isa. 19:18).§ But for its shameful treatment of the Jews in their great hour of distress, Egypt will be wholly destroyed so that for forty years it will not have an inhabitant (Ezek. 29:6–11).¶

But he shall have power over the precious things of Egypt. The treasures of Egypt will be taken out of the country and possessed by Antichrist. The rendering of the *Septuagint* is somewhat fuller: "He shall have power over the place of gold and the place of silver and over all the desire of Egypt, and the Libyans and the Ethiopians shall be in his multitude."

The *Peshitta* rendering is "And he shall have power over the house of the treasures of gold and silver, and of the pleasant things of Egypt, and the Libyans and the Cushites [Ethiopians] are his allies."

The second horseman of Revelation takes peace from the earth. Revelation does not expand this thought because Revelation is concerned with those things which connect

---

* And the Lord shall bring thee into Egypt again with ships, by the way whereof I spake unto thee, Thou shalt see it no more again: and there ye shall be sold unto your enemies for bondmen and bondwomen, and no man shall buy you. —Deut. 28:68.

§ In that day shall five cities in the land of Egypt speak the language of Canaan, and swear to the Lord of hosts; one shall be called, The city of destruction. —Isa 19:18.

¶ And all the inhabitants of Egypt shall know that I am the Lord, because they have been a staff of reed to the house of Israel. When they took hold of thee by thy hand, thou didst break, and rend all their shoulder: and when they leaned upon thee, thou brakest, and madest all their loins to be at a stand.
Therefore thus saith the Lord God; Behold, I will bring a sword upon thee, and cut off man and beast out of thee. And the land of Egypt shall be desolate and waste; and they shall know that I am the Lord: because he hath said, The river is mine, and I have made it. Behold, therefore I am against thee, and against thy rivers, and I will make the land of Egypt utterly waste and desolate, from the tower of Syene even unto the border of Ethiopia. No foot of man shall pass through it, nor foot of beast shall pass through it, neither shall it be inhabited forty years. —Ezek. 29:6–11.

with the experiences of the saints in heaven and on earth. Daniel is mostly concerned with the nations, so Daniel tells what it means to the nations to have peace taken from the earth. Jesus summed up these times by saying:

> And there shall be signs in the sun, and in the moon, and in the stars; and upon the earth distress of nations, with perplexity; the sea and the waves roaring; men's hearts failing them for fear, and for looking after those things which are coming on the earth: for the powers of heaven shall be shaken. —Luke 21:25, 26.

There are three grand phases in this process of consummation. The final goal is expressed in the only statement made from the throne in Revelation: "Behold, I make all things new." This includes the following:

1. *The redemption of the earth;* the removal of the results of sin; the purging by fire; the salvation of souls; the marriage of the Lamb; the reign of Christ.

2. *The redemption of Israel.* This is especially the subject of Ezekiel, but Ezekiel is supplemented by other prophets.

3. *The redemption of human government.* There will always be nations; man was given dominion. Satan's hold on human government will be broken and the nations will be subject to the higher government of Christ. He will rebuke strong nations afar off (Micah 4:3).* When it is all over and the saints reign from the Holy City, there will still be nations on the earth—saved nations. "The nations of them which are saved shall walk in the light of it" (the Holy City). —Rev. 21:24.

Egypt, for instance, will be totally destroyed after reaching the greatest extent of power and territory in its history, but its destruction will not be forever. The Egyptians will be scattered among the nations only for forty years, and then will return. Isaiah puts it briefly:

---

* And he shall judge among many people, and rebuke strong nations afar off; and they shall beat their swords into plowshares, and their spears into pruning-hooks: nation shall not lift up a sword against nation, neither shall they learn war any more. —Mic. 4:3.

And the Lord shall smite Egypt: he shall smite and heal it: and they shall return even to the Lord, and he shall be intreated of them, and shall heal them.

In that day shall there be a highway out of Egypt to Assyria, and the Assyrian shall come into Egypt, and the Egyptian into Assyria, and the Egyptians shall serve with the Assyrians.

In that day shall Israel be the third with Egypt and with Assyria, even a blessing in the midst of the land: whom the Lord of hosts shall bless, saying, Blessed be Egypt my people, and Assyria the work of my hands, and Israel mine inheritance. —Isa. 19:22–25.

It is not national life that will be destroyed but Satan's control of nations. God's policy is to allow evil to come to its full before judging it. Jesus announced this policy in reference to the tares: "Let both grow together until the harvest: and in the time of harvest I will say to the reapers, Gather ye together first the tares, and bind them in bundles to burn them: but gather the wheat into my barn" (Matt. 13:30).

When peace is taken from the earth, the nations will soon reach the time of harvest. Armies will be on the move. Great nations will fall. National treasurers will change hands. When the nations are in such turmoil, it will be difficult to store such vast and varied treasures as will be captured and transported from one place to another. Many of these treasures will represent works of art and other forms of precious things which must be preserved. Evidently there will be a place or house where these treasures of the nations are kept. This will fall into the hands of Antichrist.

And the Libyans and Ethiopians shall be at his steps. They shall be Antichrist's allies. When Egypt rises to power, as she will, she will reach out to take in a large section of Africa, especially North Africa. Within the new Egyptian Empire will be many provinces with as many princes (Isa. 19:11–13).* When Egypt falls, these other African peoples will be united with Antichrist.

---

* Surely the princes of Zoan are fools, the counsel of the wise counsellors of Pharaoh is become brutish: how say ye to Pharaoh, I am the son of the wise, the

HIS END COMES IN PALESTINE

But tidings out of the east and out of the north shall trouble him: therefore he shall go forth with great fury to destroy, and utterly to make away many. And he shall plant the tabernacles of his palace between the seas in the glorious holy mountain; yet he shall come to his end, and none shall help him. —Dan. 11:44, 45.

Tidings out of the east and out of the north. We have now reached the end, the time toward which all prophecy points. The final events take place around Jerusalem. It is called the Battle of Armageddon because Armageddon, on the plain of Megiddo, is the place where the armies gather. At that time the nations of the world will be aligned in two groups. The greatest number will be with Antichrist, but there will be another group of nations sufficiently strong to cause Antichrist much concern.

Palestine will be the prize, but a difficult one to obtain. Any attempt on the part of either group to enter Palestine would start a race that would include all nations.

> Behold, the day of the Lord cometh, and thy spoil shall be divided in the midst of thee. For I will gather all nations against Jerusalem to battle; and the city shall be taken, and the houses rifled, and the women ravished; and half of the city shall go forth into captivity, and the residue of the people shall not be cut off from the city. Then shall the Lord go forth, and fight against those nations, as when he fought in the day of battle.
> —Zech. 14:1-3.

This is the theme of many prophecies. Revelation also divides the nations into two groups: three sections under Antichrist and one independent. The independent group, which

son of ancient kings? Where are they? where are thy wise men? and let them tell thee now, and let them know what the Lord of hosts hath purposed upon Egypt. The princes of Zoan are become fools, the princes of Noph are deceived; they have also seduced Egypt, even they that are the stay of the tribes thereof.
—Isa. 19:11-13.

we might refer to as the Free Nations, is called in Revelation "kings of the east." In that the world is round, any nation beyond the mainland of Europe could be considered as coming from the east, especially if it had to enter Palestine from that direction. Antichrist will have the west pretty well blocked off. He will enter from the west and north; the others will have to get into Palestine from the east. They are the kings of the East.

Ezekiel has a similar grouping, only he goes into more detail concerning the identity of those nations from the east. The only countries now in existence that would fit the description are Britain, the United States, and their allies in various parts of the world (some of which have yet to become important nations). Ezekiel expresses the concern of these free nations over Antichrist's move in the direction of Palestine (Ezek. 38:13).*

He shall plant the tabernacles of his palace between the seas in the glorious holy mountain. The meaning is not that Antichrist plants his tabernacle on Mount Zion, a place of safety that Antichrist never reaches, but that he pitches his tents between the seas and Mount Zion. The troops of Antichrist will reach almost to the very foot of the holy mount. That is when Christ appears (Rev. 19).

Yet he shall come to his end. To Daniel the end of Antichrist and the beginning of the Kingdom are the same. The four visions all end on this note. The Kingdom is established without the aid of man; the Stone is cut out *without hand.* The judgment sits and the kingdom of the little horn is consumed. He stands up against the Prince of princes, but he is broken without hand. He comes to his end "and none shall help him."

---

* Sheba, and Dedan, and the merchants of Tarshish, with all the young lions thereof, shall say unto thee, Art thou come to take a spoil? hast thou gathered thy company to take a prey? to carry away silver and gold, to take away cattle and goods, to take a great spoil? —Ezek. 38:13.

SUMMARY OF THE FOUR VISIONS

Three world-empires will come and go. Then a fourth empire will rise, different from the others, which will not fall before another conqueror, but instead will break up into about ten independent countries. These countries will remain substantially intact until the time of the end.

Near the time of the end, another nation, small at the start, will become the most powerful country in Europe. The man who becomes the head of this new power will have two outstanding features—his eyes and his mouth. By what seems to be supernatural power, not his own, he will capture three countries, which were a part of the fourth empire. That will be sufficient inducement for the others to yield their sovereignty to him, and an empire is brought back into existence. To do this he will have to destroy some wonderful weapons.

From the start, this man will speak bold words against God. But now, for the first time, heaven will react violently to the words and acts of a man. Thrones will be set up in heaven, and preparations will be made to counteract what is happening on earth. The saints will now be in heaven, and there will be activity there.

On earth there will be persecution of Christians. Many will die. In Israel there will be trouble because "deals" will be made with Antichrist, gradually allowing him to get control. There will be those who understand and they will instruct many, but the persecution will be severe and many will die because of it.

Meantime, wars will break out all over the world. Many great nations will fall, but Antichrist will remain in control of most of the world. In the end, he will hear reports from distant lands that will cause him to make a sudden drive against Israel.

Then God's kingdom will be established. All of Anti-christ's armies along with Antichrist himself will be destroyed. The saints will possess the kingdom.

Study 9

"THE TIME OF THE END"
Daniel 12

"THE TIME OF THE END"
Daniel 12

"THE TIME OF THE END"

And at that time shall Michael stand up, the great prince which standeth for the children of thy people: and there shall be a time of trouble, such as never was since there was a nation even to that same time: and at that time thy people shall be delivered, every one that shall be found written in the book. —Dan. 12:1.

The Peshitta rendering of this verse is this: "At that time shall stand up Michael, the great angel who is overseer over the children of thy people, and it shall be a time of affliction such as has not been from the days of eternity; there shall be delivered of the children of thy people every one who is found written in the book."

At that time. Commentators are at a loss to understand why the end of Antichrist's reign (when he comes to his end and no one comes to his aid) should begin a time of trouble such as never was. It seems that this should be a time of joy, not of affliction. *The Pulpit Commentary* remarks on these words: "It seems as if the connection here was hopelessly broken; some dislocation has occurred." But the "dislocation" is in our understanding the prophetic method. "At the time of the end" is a formula (with variations) used as

241

an indicator of time. It has no reference to what has just been said. It does not point back but rather looks forward to the appointed time of the end. The "time of the end," "that day," and "the day of the Lord" all refer to the general time of the final fulfillment of prophecy. The use of any one of these terms indicates that the previous subject has been brought to a close, and some new phase of that time is about to be taken up.

The standard prophetic method is at first to leave out all details that would tend to confuse, and then to put these in at the end. (Jesus followed this same method in the Olivet Discourse—that is, *after* He had completed the main narrative, He stated the details of the Rapture.) In Daniel 12, the particular feature about to be amplified is the Rapture, which Daniel had already referred to in three of his visions (Chapter 7, 8, 10–11). But there was no opportunity then to go into detail. And so, in Daniel 12, the phrase *at that time* merely means that now new details are to be filled in.

Shall Michael stand up. Michael is "the archangel"— the only one so named in the Bible.* He seems to be the one who commands the armed forces of heaven. Whenever he is mentioned, there is something to be done requiring force. His most prominent place is in connection with resurrection, for it was he who contended with Satan about the body of Moses. When Satan contested Moses' resurrection, Michael had to take a hand. The fact that Moses was raised from the dead is evidenced by his appearance on the Mount of Transfiguration in his glorified body, along with Elijah, who was "caught up." Thus there will be two witnesses to the promise of resurrection: one representing those who will be "caught up," and one representing those who will be "raised up" from the dead.

---

* Yet Michael the archangel, when contending with the devil he disputed about the body of Moses, durst not bring against him a railing accusation, but said, The Lord rebuke thee. —Jude 9.

Three signals will announce the Rapture: the shout, the trumpet, and *the voice of the archangel, Michael* (I Thess. 4:16).* As usual, Michael will be there because there will be opposition to be overcome. But if Satan in past days so opposed the resurrection of *one* man, Moses, then he will use his whole power to try to prevent the resurrection of *all* the saints. All the principalities and powers of darkness in high places will be mobilized to keep the new bodies of the saints from passing through. Revelation says that Satan will muster one-third of the angels; to counter this force will be poised not just Michael, but Michael and all his angels. The story is told so vividly in Revelation that it needs no comment.

> And there was war in heaven: Michael *and his angels* fought against the dragon; and the dragon fought and his angels, and prevailed not; neither was their place found any more in heaven. And the great dragon was cast out, that old serpent, called the Devil, and Satan, which deceiveth the whole world: he was cast out into the earth, and his angels were cast out with him.
>
> And I heard a loud voice saying in heaven, Now is come salvation, and strength, and the kingdom of our God, and the power of his Christ: for the accuser of our brethren is cast down, which accused them before our God day and night. And they overcame him by the blood of the Lamb, and by the word of their testimony; and they loved not their lives unto the death.
>
> Therefore rejoice, ye heavens, and ye that dwell in them. Woe to the inhabiters of the earth and of the sea! for the devil is come down unto you, having great wrath, because he knoweth that he hath but a short time.
> —Rev. 12:7–12.

The Resurrection has a double result: not only is heaven filled with saints with their new bodies, but Satan is cast out and must now operate on the earth as a man. When

---

* For the Lord himself shall descend from heaven with a shout, with the voice of the archangel, and with the trump of God: and the dead in Christ shall rise first. —I Thess. 4:16.

Daniel wrote the following, he too saw the saints in heaven and Satan cast out:

> I beheld till the thrones were cast down, and the Ancient of days did sit, whose garment was white as snow, and the hair of his head like the pure wool: his throne was like the fiery flame, and his wheels as burning fire.
> A fiery stream issued and came forth from before him: thousand thousands ministered unto him, and ten thousand times ten thousand stood before him: the judgment was set, and the books were opened. I beheld then because of the voice of the great words which the horn spake: I beheld even till the beast was slain, and his body destroyed and given to the burning flame.
> —Dan. 7:9–11.

At the time of Daniel Chapter 7, the details of the Rapture had to be left out. Daniel saw the saints in heaven, but there was no occasion to tell how they got there; now in Chapter 12 we have added details concerning "that time."

The children of thy people. It is possible to jump to the conclusion that "the children of Daniel's people" would have to be the Jews. But the fact is that in these four visions of Gentile world-power, the Jews are hardly noticed. Chapter 9 alone is devoted to Israel; the four visions are not. Daniel's "people" are the saints in *all* dispensations and are the ones Daniel is talking about when he says:

> And the kingdom and dominion, and the greatness of the kingdom under the whole heaven, shall be given to *the people of the saints of the most High*, whose kingdom is an everlasting kingdom, and all dominions shall serve and obey him. —Dan. 7:27.

It is not the Jews on earth that will possess the kingdom, but the overcomers in the Church who are in heaven after the Rapture.

> And he that overcometh, and keepth my works unto the end, to him will I give power over the nations: and

he shall rule them with a rod of iron; as the vessels of a potter shall they be broken to shivers: even as I received of my Father. —Rev. 2:26, 27.

It is the saints, not the Jews, who are to be kings and priests. Daniel's "people" are God's people. The Jews as a nation will have no part in the Rapture; they will be redeemed only after the return of Christ—that is, after, not before, this time of trouble. The saints will be kept out of the time of trouble by the Rapture, as was revealed to Daniel. In Daniel 12 we are told the reason for the Rapture; it is to deliver God's people from the impending judgment.

There shall be a time of trouble, such as never was since there was a nation, says Daniel. Jesus quotes this in Matthew 24:21* and adds, "No, nor ever shall be." There could be only one such time, for the next time it would not be a time of trouble such as never was; therefore, Jesus and Daniel must be talking about the same time. Again we approach a subject that is well developed in prophecy, for this "time of trouble" is given a great deal of space in Scripture. It differs from other times of distress in five important respects:

a. It is "world-wide." For that reason, there is no escape.

Fear, and the pit, and the snare, are upon thee, O inhabitant of *the earth*. And it shall come to pass, that he who fleeth from the noise of the fear shall fall into the pit; and he that cometh up out of the midst of the pit shall be taken in the snare: for the windows from on high are open, and the foundations of the earth do shake.

The earth is utterly broken down, *the earth* is clean dissolved, *the earth* is moved exceedingly. *The earth* shall reel to and fro like a drunkard, and shall be removed like a cottage; and the transgression thereof shall be heavy upon it; and it shall fall, and not rise again. —Isa. 24:17–20.

* For then shall be great tribulation, such as was not since the beginning of the world to this time, no, nor ever shall be. —Matt. 24:21.

b. It is "a judgment." It is called a harvest, a time of separation, of punishment and reward.

> And it shall come to pass in that day, that the Lord *shall punish the host of the high ones that are on high,* and the kings of the earth upon the earth. And they shall be gathered together, as prisoners are gathered in the pit, and shall be shut up in the prison, and after many days shall they be visited.
>
> Then the moon shall be confounded, and the sun ashamed, when the Lord of hosts shall reign in mount Zion, and in Jerusalem, and before his ancients gloriously. —Isa 24:21–23.

God always acts to save His people from a time of judgment—that is, judgment imposed from above, not judgment that is the usual course of nature. Before sending the Flood, God prepared an ark of safety for the one righteous family. Before destroying Sodom, God sent His angel to deliver Lot, and the angel's statement on that occasion expressed a basic truth or policy upon which God operates: "Haste thee, escape thither: for I cannot do any thing till thou be come thither."

Judgment is for sinners, and it is not God's policy to send it on the righteous. In a sense, God could not do so because such judgment is a punishment for sin, and that price was paid by Christ on the cross. God could not punish people for their sins after Christ had atoned for them; therefore God's people must be taken out of the world *before* that kind of judgment can strike. There is coming a time of trouble such as never was, but God's people will be delivered.

This same truth is found in the message to the church in Philadelphia: "Because thou hast kept the word of my patience, I also will keep thee from the hour of temptation, which shall come upon all the world, to try them that dwell upon the earth" (Rev. 3:10). "That dwell upon the earth" is in contrast with those who, after the Rapture, dwell in heaven. "Therefore rejoice, ye heavens, and ye that dwell in them. Woe to the inhabiters of the earth and of the sea! for the devil is come down unto you, having great wrath, because he knoweth that he hath but a short time" (Rev. 12:12).

c. It is "administered from heaven." That is why thrones are set up and "the Ancient of days" sits. The seven last plagues are all sent and controlled by agents from heaven.

d. The judgment includes Satan and his angels. One of the reasons why this is a time of trouble "such as never was, or ever will be" is that the earth becomes the scene of the final conflict with Satan. Demons, held in prison for ages, are turned loose upon the earth. A thing like this can never happen again.

e. It is "the time of the end." This means much more than the words might suggest. It is not only the end of a dispensation. It is the end of a whole series of dispensations, the end of a conflict and program begun in ages past. Neither earth nor heaven will be the same again.

And at that time thy people shall be delivered, every one that shall be found written in the book. Inasmuch as there can be only one such time of trouble, so there can be only one such deliverance—the Rapture. The word *deliver* here means rescue—to rescue from impending danger. Here we have the clearest statement of the reason for the Rapture; it is to save God's people from the time of trouble.

THE RESURRECTION

And many of them that sleep in the dust of the earth shall awake, some to everlasting life, and some to shame and everlasting contempt. —Dan. 12:2.

If we did not already know that Daniel is talking about the Resurrection, we would know it now. Sleep as a synonym of death is frequent in both the Old and New Testaments. "Now is Christ risen from the dead, and become the firstfruits of them that slept" (I Cor. 15: 20).

Them that sleep in the dust. Sleep is a physical function. This reference about sleep, as in all references to the Resurrection, is to the body, which reposes in dust, not to the spirit, which as far as we know does not sleep. Although almost all details of the Rapture may be found in essence in the Old Testament, it required the New Testament to bring them into focus. David prayed, "I shall be satisfied, when I awake, with thy likeness" (Ps. 17: 15).

In I Corinthians 15, Paul closes his great discourse on the Resurrection with two references to the Old Testament of which he says the Resurrection is a fulfillment.

> So when this corruptible shall have put on incorruption, and this mortal shall have put on immortality, then shall be brought to pass the saying that is written, Death is swallowed up in victory. O death, where is thy sting? O grave, where is thy victory? —I Cor. 15: 54, 55.

"Death is swallowed up in victory." This phrase is quoted by Paul from Isaiah 25: 8: "He will swallow up death in victory; and the Lord God will wipe away tears from off all faces; and the rebuke of his people shall he take away from off all the earth: for the Lord hath spoken it." The phrase, "O death, where is thy sting? O grave, where is thy victory?" is quoted by Paul from Hosea 13: 14: "I will ransom them from the power of the grave; I will redeem them from death: O death, I will be thy plagues; O grave, I will be thy destruction."

Like Daniel, Isaiah has the saints gathered to a place of safety during the time of trouble; and, like Paul, Isaiah has the dead raised first. The Authorized Version has an unfortunate translation. When you read Isaiah 26: 19–21, you should omit the italicized words, *men* and *together with*, which are not in the original, and also you should note that the word *body* is plural. The passage, "The dead men shall live, together with my dead body shall they arise," *should* read thus:

> Thy dead shall live; my dead *bodies* shall arise. Awake and sing, ye that dwell in dust: for thy dew is as the dew of herbs, and the earth shall cast out the dead.
>
> Come, my people, enter thou into thy chambers, and shut thy doors about thee: hide thyself as it were for a little moment, until the indignation be overpast. For, behold, the Lord cometh out of his place to punish the inhabitants of the earth for their iniquity: the earth also shall disclose her blood, and shall no more cover her slain. —Isa. 26:19–21.

Some [awake] to everlasting life, and some to shame and everlasting contempt. This is not a general resurrection of all the dead, for "many [not all] of them that sleep in the dust shall arise." This verse refers to the resurrection at the Rapture. Why, then, does it include "some to shame and everlasting contempt"?

Here we need a careful and much more detailed study of Scripture. As we gain more information, we have to enlarge our conception of future things. Most people seem to do the reverse; they try to confine all new revelations to their small knowledge. (Scientists are continually broadening their horizons; Bible students should do the same.) In comparison with the abundance of revelation, there is no field of prophecy where our knowledge of Scripture is so restricted as in the matter of the Resurrection. For the most part, we have been taught only the bare essentials, but actually, the Resurrection is a very complex event, involving the following: the dead "in Christ"; the dead who have had an opportunity to be saved; the living saints; the fallen angels; Michael and his angels; Satan, who will be cast out of heaven; Christ, who will descend from heaven with a shout; God, whose trumpet will sound. In fact, all creation seems to be concerned with the grandest event in prophecy.

The two groups specially in view in Daniel 12:2 are these: first, the dead in Christ who will be raised; and second, those who had been connected with the saints but had died unsaved. Here is revealed a truth that, if made known, would shake the Church to its foundations. It will undoubtedly be a factor in the last days of the Church. It deals with the most powerful evangelistic truth in prophecy—the fate of the almost Christian. Let us study this phase of our subject in minute detail.

In our minds we divide humanity into groups: the saved and the lost. Actually, there are three general groups: first, the saved; then the lost; and finally the almost saved. Or, to put it in another way, we may divide the lost into two groups: those who had no opportunity, and those who are completely responsible because they lived among Christians. In this latter group are many who think they will be saved.

This is one of the most terrifying things in prophecy—the anguish of those who were "pillars in the church," but unsaved. Jesus spent so much time talking about these people that one might think it preyed on His mind. It is the saddest situation He had to face. Many of His parables are warnings of this terrifying fate of the almost Christian. Each time Jesus warned "there shall be weeping and gnashing of teeth" (seven times in all), He was telling about the separation *at the Rapture* of those who had lived among the saved, or who—because of their race, or religion, or family, or morals, or standing in the community, or good works—just assumed they were saved.

For instance, when the Gentile centurion showed more faith than the Jews, Jesus took the occasion to issue His first warning to *those who were depending upon their race*:

> When Jesus heard it, he marvelled, and said to them that followed, Verily I say unto you, I have not found so great faith, no, not in Israel. And I say unto you, That many shall come from the east and west, and

shall sit down with Abraham, and Isaac, and Jacob, in the kingdom of heaven. But *the children of the kingdom* shall be cast out into outer darkness: there shall be weeping and gnashing of teeth. —Matt. 8:10–12.

Again, to those who are *depending on their standing in the community,* Jesus said:

When once the master of the house is risen up, and hath shut to the door, and ye begin to stand without, and to knock at the door, saying, Lord, Lord, open unto us; and he shall answer and say unto you, I know you not whence ye are: then shall ye begin to say, *We have eaten and drunk in thy presence, and thou hast taught in our streets.*

But he shall say, I tell you, I know you not whence ye are; depart from me, all ye workers of iniquity. There shall be weeping and gnashing of teeth, when ye shall see Abraham, and Isaac, and Jacob, and all the prophets, in the kingdom of God, and you yourselves thrust out. —Luke 13:25–28.

Notice that Jesus says, "Ye shall *see* Abraham, and Isaac, and Jacob." These people who "see" are *not* sleeping; they are there, right on the very threshhold of the kingdom; they even try to get in, but are "thrust out." Please note this one point carefully: *Neither Daniel nor Jesus was talking about those living on the earth at the time of the Rapture.* Such people would not be expected to see Abraham and Isaac and Jacob and all the prophets enter the kingdom. As far as the living unsaved are concerned, they will just not be caught up. Their final judgment will come later. God will *not* cast people into outer darkness nor into the furnace of fire while they are still living on the earth. *Judgment will come only after death,* for "it is appointed unto men once to die, but *after this* the judgment" (Heb. 9:27).

Let us first examine two Scriptures concerning those living on earth at the time of the Rapture. Among those living will be some "taken," but some "left." In dealing with the living who remain, Jesus did not consign them to outer darkness; they are simply left to go into the tribulation. For example, in Matthew 25 we have the parable of the ten virgins:

> And at midnight there was a cry made, Behold, the bridegroom cometh; go ye out to meet him. Then all those virgins arose, and trimmed their lamps. And the foolish said unto the wise, Give us of your oil; for our lamps are gone out. But the wise answered, saying, Not so; . . . but go ye. . . , and buy for yourselves.
>
> And while they went to buy, the bridegroom came; and they that were ready went in with him to the marriage: *and the door was shut.* Afterward came also the other virgins, saying, Lord, Lord, open to us. But he answered and said, Verily I say unto you, *I know you not.* —Matt. 25:6–12.

Among those living at the coming of the Bridegroom, two groups are represented—five wise and five foolish. But note that there is no word of condemnation for the five foolish virgins. They simply did *not* go in.

Likewise the evil servant who said, "My lord delayeth his "coming," was appointed a place among the hypocrites—for he *was* a hypocrite.

> If that evil servant shall say in his heart, My lord delayeth his coming; and shall begin to smite his fellowservants, and to eat and drink with the drunken; the lord of that servant shall come in a day when he looketh not for him, and in an hour that he is not aware of, and shall cut him asunder, and appoint him his *portion with the hypocrites:* there shall be weeping and gnashing of teeth. —Matt. 24:48–51.

He was a servant; he held a high position in the church; he was closely connected with the kingdom; he even knew about and believed in the Second Coming of Christ—yet he was not a believer. (This is the only time when referring to people who are still living that Jesus says, "There shall be weeping and gnashing of teeth.") This evil servant probably represents a large number of church members at the time of the Rapture who are active enough to be called servants and yet are unsaved. The evil servant separated himself—angels did not come down and cast him out, nor is anything said about "outer darkness" or the "furnace of fire." This man was still living; his judgment was yet to come after he died.

Jesus is the only prophet who had a clear picture of the Resurrection in all of its phases. While other prophets had a vision of the scene *on this earth,* Jesus saw how the *spirit world* would be affected. He saw *the dead stirred* by the Resurrection, and by many illustrations revealed the whole situation to us. But most of us are reluctant to accept His statements, which are not what we have been led to believe.

Let us compare the general belief with the teachings of Jesus. We Christians have usually supposed that in the final judgment day there will be just two classes of people, saved and lost. But the fact is that there will be degrees of punishment and reward. The decisive factor will be *opportunity,* and with opportunity will come responsibility. In Matthew 25:14–30, the servant who received two talents was given the same reward as the one who had five talents. Why? Because he had made equal use of his opportunity. The man who received one talent was considered one of the servants, but he went and hid his Lord's money, making no use of it; therefore he was cast out. He did nothing, so he lost everything. Both the rewards *and* the punishment were based on the use or misuse of opportunity.

On this basis we can classify the unsaved on the judgment day as follows: first, those who have had an opportunity because they heard; second, those who have had no opportunity because they have never heard. Jesus talked much about the ones who had heard—especially those who had actually lived among Christians but were never saved. These people, He said, would be judged *not* according to their works *but* for their lack of faith. Thus those who had heard the Word and not received it would be judged by their unbelief.

On the other hand, those who have *not* heard will be judged by their works. Faith comes *"by hearing,"* but those who have never heard, and therefore who have had no opportunity to exercise faith, will be judged according to their works. There will be no other basis for the judgment at the great white throne (Rev. 20:11–15).

At the time of the Rapture the number who will be living will be small *compared with the millions that have come and gone.* As we said before, when Jesus looked forward to the Rapture, *it was of these untold millions* He was thinking and spoke. Let us consider in more detail three of Jesus' parables, dealing especially with *those who had an opportunity*—that is, with the dead who had once lived among Christians. In each parable, this group was *closely connected* with the kingdom. First, then, in the parable of the tares Jesus said,

> As therefore the tares are gathered and burned in the fire; so shall it be in the end of this world. The Son of man shall send forth his angels, and they shall gather *out of his kingdom* all things that offend, and them which do iniquity; and shall cast them into a furnace of fire: there shall be wailing and gnashing of teeth. —Matt. 13:40–42.

Likewise in the parable of the fish in the net:

> The kingdom of heaven is like unto a net, that was cast into the sea, and gathered of every kind: which, when it was full, they drew to shore, and sat down, and gathered the good into vessels, but cast the bad away. So shall it be at the end of the world: the angels shall come forth, and sever the wicked *from among the just*, and shall cast them into the furnace of fire: there shall be wailing and gnashing of teeth. —Matt. 13:47–50.

The bad fish are "in" the kingdom in one sense—they are *in* the net along with the good fish and expect to go into the eternal kingdom along with the saved. But they will be disappointed. Their separation will come; it will come at the Rapture.

Lastly, the "man who had not on a wedding garment" resembles one who tries to "crash the kingdom" by his own works. At the coming of the King, he will be disgraced in front of his friends and relatives.

> Those servants went out. . . , and gathered together. . . , both bad and good: and the wedding was furnished with guests. And when the king came in to see the guests, he saw there a man which had not on a wedding garment: and he saith unto him, Friend, how camest thou in hither not having a wedding garment? And he was speechless.
>
> Then said the king to the servants, Bind him hand and foot, and *take him away, and cast him into outer darkness;* there shall be weeping and gnashing of teeth. For many are called, but few are chosen. —Matt. 22:10–14.

This scene could *not* be connected with the "great white throne" judgment, for the white throne judgment will come long after the saints have received their rewards and are reigning with Christ. *The separation, that is, the judgment for unbelief, must be made long before this—at the time of the Rapture.* This judgment of the man without a wedding garment will be a final judgment. At the great white throne there will be two sets of books and two classes of people. First of all, there will be those who had never heard and who therefore had no personal responsibility. These will be judged according to their works as written in the books: "The dead were judged out of those things which were written in the books, according to their works" (Rev. 20:12). But some will have been crossed out of the book of life because they have already been judged. These are the unbelievers who were cast out at the Rapture, and who now without further ceremony will be cast into the lake of fire.

What the angel told Daniel, therefore, is exactly right: "*Many* of them that sleep in the dust of the earth shall awake, *some* to everlasting life, *and some* to shame and everlasting contempt."

A COMING REVIVAL

And they that be wise shall shine as the brightness of the firmament; and they that turn many to righteousness as the stars for ever and ever. —Dan. 12:3.

And they that be wise, or "they that understand" (as it is rendered in many versions). A very large part of the Bible is prophecy, much of which has *never* been understood and in fact has been pretty much disregarded. But God has said, "My word ... that goeth forth out of my mouth ... shall not return unto me void, but ... it shall prosper in the thing whereto I sent it" (Isa. 55:11). The prophetic Scriptures have been specially prepared for a given time, and when that time comes, there will be those who understand. These will instruct many and turn many to righteousness. Prophecy will have a powerful evangelistic appeal when its time has come.

KNOWLEDGE IS POWER

But thou, O Daniel, shut up the words, and seal the book, even to the time of the end: many shall run to and fro, and knowledge shall be increased. —Dan. 12:4.

O Daniel, shut up the words and seal the book, even to the time of the end. A sermonette in a well-known paper began by saying, "I have plowed through the prophetic books of the Bible several times and have found wondrous nuggets here and there, but on the whole, Jeremiah, Ezekiel, Obadiah, Micah, Nahum, Habakkuk, and others seemed tedious and dull."

Although not all readers are as frank to say it, that is the way these prophecies strike most readers. But these and the other prophetic books contain more than nuggets. They are packed full of marvels of more current interest than anything in the newspapers or news magazines. Yet their time has not yet come, for "until the time of the end," the prophecy is "closed up" and sealed.

Many shall run to and fro. There are two essentials to a wide dissemination of truth: first, a revelation of the truth; next, a desire to know the truth. The revelation of truth came a long time ago, for God's campaign against Satan is a planned campaign, and every detail has already been worked out.

If Satan can discover God's strategy, he always copies it. For the last days, he has even anticipated God's program of information contained in the prophetic Scriptures. Many of his false religions are based on Bible prophecies. Even false Christs will say, "The time draweth near." Yet there is one difference: God's prophecies will come true.

The key to the phrase "many shall run to and fro" is in the word *many*. A *few* people are interested now (there have always been a few), but in the last days *many* shall run to and fro. "Runners" were those who carried messages. "I have not sent these prophets, yet they ran" (Jer. 23:21). To run is to proclaim. This whole phrase "is not referring to the modern rapidity of locomotion, as some think. But whereas now *few* care for this prophecy of God, at the time of the end, near its fulfillment, *many* shall run to and fro— i.e., scrutinize it, running through every page." —Faussett. So the angel told Daniel to shut up the words, and seal the book, even to the time of the end; then, at the right time, many shall run to and fro, and the knowledge which Daniel desired will be made known universally.

"We here reach the 'consummation of all things.' This section is to be looked upon as a description of the last time, when circumstances shall remove the seal from the book. The verb translated *going to and fro* may be rendered *to peruse*. When men peruse the prophecy carefully and knowledge is increased, the veil shall then be removed and the seals broken." —*Pulpit Commentary*.

Knowledge shall be increased. Presidents today have to decide issues never before dreamed of by former presidents or rulers, and a new president not only begins a new term of office but a new epoch, marked by radical changes. Actually it is science, not Russia, that is changing the world. From the standpoint of prophecy, Russia is a passing phase hardly worthy of note. Russia can only threaten and terrorize the world, not conquer or destroy it. Some prophecies do seem to refer to Russia or at least to Communism. (Ezekiel 38 is not one of them.) These indicate that Russia as a nation will be totally destroyed by the rise of Antichrist.

Russia may only terrorize the world; Antichrist will amaze the world. The feature of his rise that will be so world-shaking will be his connection with the spirit world. If the truth about flying saucers were made known, the people *might* be prepared for what is coming; but as it is, they are unprepared and the shock will be very great.

Russia will have *atomic power;* Antichrist will have *satanic power.* His coming will be "after the working of Satan, with all power and signs and lying wonders." Were it not for the fact that God also has a strategy, Satan's impact on the world would be decisive and overwhelming. The backbone of this strategy is Bible prophecy. God says, "Behold, I have told you *before.*" By revealing Satan's operations in advance, God will take the edge off them. Certainly the One who can accurately predict everything that Satan will do will have a greater influence than Satan and his agents. This strategy is announced in Isaiah:

> Remember the former things of old: for I am God, and there is none else; I am God, and there is none like me, *declaring the end from the beginning,* and from ancient times the things that are not yet done, saying, My counsel shall stand, and I will do all my pleasure: . . .

yea, I have spoken it, I will also bring it to pass; I have purposed it, I will also do it. —Isa. 46:9-11.

Because God's advance information was written not *just* before but *thousands of years* before its fulfillment, it will be the more effective. The difficulties encountered in writing history so far in advance were enormous—principally because language is so fickle and living conditions change from generation to generation. To tell of things that would not come into view for two or three thousand years, new words had to be continually invented to name new things—words unknown, of course, to the prophets. Automobiles are "chariots"; airplanes are "horses with wheels like a whirlwind"; a dictator is a "vile person, to whom they will not give the honour of the kingdom."

There will not be a continuous improvement in world conditions until peace is made permanent. A contest began in the Garden of Eden and will end in the account given in Revelation—a contest for possession and control of the world by "principalities and powers in the heavenly places." In the last days when the full force of this contest strikes, there will be "a time of trouble such as never was." Satan will be fighting on all fronts, using every means at his disposal. False Christs will multiply, and a great effort will be made to win people. (After all, it is the population of the earth, not the physical things, that is important. God can make new worlds, but He cannot create a redeemed people.)

Satan will be able to produce great signs and wonders, but there is one miracle that Satan can *not* duplicate—he can not foretell the future. Prophecy seems today to be a speculative thing, for there are many divergent voices, and prophetic teachers are not in too good repute. That is because the time is not right. It is said, "There is nothing as powerful as a truth when its time has come; prior to that time, a truth may be ridiculed and its preachers persecuted." The fulfillment of prophecy, then, will do two things at once:

unseal the book, and create a demand for the knowledge contained in the prophetic Scriptures. Here is God's strategy for the grand climax of history. (Its importance may be judged by the amount of space given to it in the Bible.)

This is one of the marvelous things about prophecy. It is the mainstay of God's strategy and is *for the last days*. Thousands of years before it would be used, it was written and published. If it had been understood all those years, it would have lost its impact on the world in the last days. Prophecy was written in such a way that through the years it contained only nuggets, but at the proper time it will suddenly come to life with the most sensational pronouncements of all time. By telling Satan's plans in advance, God will frustrate them.

All the churches will be watching the prophetic Scripture, and their predictions will be common knowledge. This indicates that there will be some terrific changes in the make-up of the Church, for today prophecies concerning the part the Church will play in the days ahead have been almost entirely overlooked. Judgment must begin at the house of God, for the Church is not ready for the task ahead—the most strenuous task it has ever faced. No changes coming upon society and the nations will be more revolutionary than those scheduled for the Church.

The churches are not interested today in God's program (except as it may be twisted to benefit the individual society or denomination). Sermons are made up of trivia. A Scripture text may be used to introduce a sermon, but the rest of the sermon gives the opinions of men. Sunday school teaching is the same. The Scriptures are not expounded today; therefore there is widespread ignorance of the basic redemption truths. This is not the fault of the preachers, for it goes deeper than that. The schools have not given the preachers the preparation they paid for. The churches are run like big business concerns in competition with each other, each one trying to put out what the people want. Their driving motive is increase in membership and material gain.

But all this will change. The realization of the nearness of the Kingdom will work amazing changes in the attitudes of the people. They will want more information and less nice talk. "Knowledge will be increased." This could also bring about a change in the very organization of the church. We might call the new church the Kingdom Church.

THE KINGDOM CHURCH

The Kingdom Church! This sounds like a strange combination of words—kingdom and church. That is only because of our historic misuse of Bible words. It is true that the Kingdom of David will again be set up in Jerusalem and will be an everlasting kingdom. But in the New Testament, the term *kingdom* has no reference to the Kingdom of David. The "kingdom of heaven" is not the Davidic Kingdom. It may include the Kingdom of David, but goes far beyond it.

The Kingdom of Heaven is the grandest conception of an infinite God. It exceeds the powers of man's mind so far that its very principles seem like contradictions. It cannot easily be defined, for its extent is so great, its coverage so universal, that to contain it in a definition seems impossible. (To define an infinite thing is itself a contradiction in terms.)

Maybe you think the Church cannot be changed. But Luther changed the Church; the Wesleyan movement changed the Church; and the rise of Antichrist, with his satanic power, will change the nations and the world to an extent never before dreamed of. To counteract Satan and the host of false prophets, God will turn loose the power of His Word, which has been "kept in store" since the foundations of the world. Here is something more powerful than anything Luther or Wesley ever possessed, and do you not think it will change the Church?

Prophetic time from now till the millennium may be divided into three parts: (1) from now till the Rapture; (2) from the Rapture till the Resurrection of the tribulation saints (which completes the first resurrection); and (3) the seven last plagues. The amount of prophecy pointed at the period from now till the Rapture is greater than usually suspected. (A tendency on the part of Christians to want the Rapture immediately causes some wishful thinking, which sometimes blinds us to the actual facts.) The Church still has a ways to go. It still has a job to do. Its final phase is still ahead.

The book of Revelation (which was not written just to fill up space in the Bible) will turn out to be the Church's greatest book. It is the doorway into all prophecy. Until the Church has taken the place assigned to it in Daniel and Revelation, there will be no Rapture. In both Daniel and Revelation it is made clear that to be "caught up" the Church will have to be not an ignorant Church but a watching Church. But when we compare the present state of the Church's Bible knowledge with the vast amount of revelation in the prophetic Scriptures, the only word that can be applied to the Church is ignorance. This ignorance will have to change.

A SWORN STATEMENT

Then I Daniel looked, and behold, there stood other two, the one on this side of the bank of the river, and the other on that side of the bank of the river. And one said to the man clothed in linen, which was upon the waters of the river, How long shall it be to the end of these wonders?

And I heard the man clothed in linen, which was upon the waters of the river, when he held up his right hand and his left hand unto heaven, and sware by him that liveth for ever that it shall be for a time, times, and an half; and when he shall have accomplished to scatter the power of the holy people, all these things shall be finished. —Dan. 12:5–7.

He held up his right hand and his left hand unto heaven and sware. Daniel is the only prophetic book that ends with an affidavit, a *sworn* statement. (Revelation ends with a *signed* statement: "I Jesus have sent mine angel to testify unto you these things in the churches.") Although the entire book of Daniel may thus be considered as verified, the affidavit particularly concerns Chapter 11, which stands out as one of the most important chapters in prophecy. It starts with the most elaborate introduction of any prophecy in the Bible and ends with the most solemn pronouncement of its truth. It is a revelation of "that which is noted in the scripture of truth." There seems to have been a heavenly record of what is to happen, of which Daniel 11 is only a copy. It is to the accuracy of this copy that the angel swares. When the time is fulfilled, the copy will speak with an authority and a demonstration of power that will startle the world and revive the Church.

Watch these prophetic chapters in Daniel for the spark that will light the torch for the Church in the last days, for these chapters contain things kept secret from the foundation of the world; they are prepared and preserved for the grandest days of the Church's history. When Satan makes his all-out bid for control of the world and the Church, he will be balked by the fact that his strategy has been revealed in advance. The Church has it.

A time, times, and an half (1260 days). This is the first of three periods of about 3½ years each. (The other two are mentioned later in vs. 11 and 12.) This symbolic way of expressing time is explained in two verses in Revelation 12, where the same time period is given in days, as well as in symbol:

> To the woman were given two wings of a great eagle, that she might fly into the wilderness, into her place, where she is nourished for *a time, and times, and half a time*, from the face of the serpent (vs. 14). The woman

fled into the wilderness, where she hath a place prepared of God, that they should feed her there *a thousand two hundred and threescore days* (vs. 6).

Time equals one year; *times* equals two years; *half a time* equals one-half year. Therefore 1260 days equals 3½ years. One reason for expressing time symbolically as well as in actual days is so that the days could not be taken for so many years. (Some people do this anyway.) The time element in the verse we are studying (Dan. 12: 7) refers back to Daniel Chapter 7: "He shall speak great words against the most High, . . . and think to change times and laws: and they shall be given into his hand until *a time* and *times* and *the dividing of time*" (Dan. 7: 25).

The holy people. These are the tribulation saints. When Antichrist has disposed of them, these final events will take place immediately.

THE END OF THESE THINGS

And I heard, but I understood not: then said I, O my Lord, what shall be the end of these things? And he said, Go thy way, Daniel: for the words are closed up and sealed till the time of the end. Many shall be purified, and made white, and tried; but the wicked shall do wickedly: and none of the wicked shall understand; but the wise shall understand.
—Dan. 12:8–10.

The words were closed up and sealed. The words were *not* concealed but published. But their meaning was "closed up" to wait for their fulfillment. Like many other prophecies in the Bible, the prophecies of Daniel are known but not understood because they are too far removed from the accomplishment. When the time approaches, events will aid the understanding.

None of the wicked shall understand but the wise shall understand.

Not everyone will understand. To enlighten the understanding will take the event plus the operation of the Spirit. In the last days many false prophets will seem to have an explanation. Probably Daniel will then be quoted more than any other book. Yet truths in Daniel can and will be known only by those who have the mind of Christ.

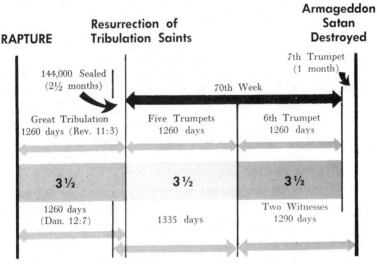

The only differences between the length of the times given here in Daniel and those given elsewhere are the time required to seal the 144,000, and the time required for the 7th trumpet.

1290 DAYS AND 1335 DAYS

And from the time that the daily sacrifice shall be taken away, and the abomination that maketh desolate set up, there shall be a thousand two hundred and ninety days. Blessed is he that waiteth, and cometh to the thousand three hundred and five and thirty days. —Dan. 12:11, 12.

A thousand two hundred and ninety days. Mentioned in this closing chapter are three periods of approximately 3½ years each. The first, as we have stated, is given in a

symbolical manner, "a time, times, and an half" (vs. 7),
and represents about 3½ years; it is in fact 3½ years of
360 days each. That would be 3½ years minus 18 days.

Let me add here that it may be that the original year
was 360 days; a year today is 365 days; in the future, after
the convulsions of nature noted in Revelation and Isaiah,
it may again be 360 days. The purpose of prophecy is not to
pinpoint the time to the very minute; in fact, that would be
impossible in many cases because events do not move that
fast. For instance, you might say that a war lasted four
years, but the exact time of the start (down to the day)
might be either when the first shot was fired or when the
declaration of war was issued. Even so, the end of the war
might be considered as either when the last shot was fired,
or when the armistice was made, or when the treaty of
peace was signed. This might make a difference of a few
days or even months.

And so, in all prophecies, these times are about the same
length of days, but there may be some slight variation between those relating to the Jews and those relating to the
nations. For instance, to the saints, the Second Coming of
Christ may be when He comes in the clouds with His saints,
as recorded in Revelation 19. But to the nations, the Second
Coming may be when He destroys Antichrist. (Daniel saw it
that way.) And to the Jews, the Second Coming will be
when He comes suddenly to His temple, according to Malachi.
These events will be a few days apart. Ezekiel's time of 2520
years (Ezekiel 4) may even run to the formal establishing
of the kingdom. Daniel's final "week" could begin and end
with any number of important events which will happen
during that time. The last week of 7 years is divided into two
parts, though they may not be exactly equal. Daniel 9 says,
"in the midst of the week." This would not have to be the
exact center down to the day but somewhere near the
middle.

And so, a difference of a few days or weeks in two different reckonings would only mean that we have a different starting or stopping point for each particular situation. The fact remains that Daniel was given three separate, unequal periods of about 3½ years each. (The same three periods may be determined by a study of Revelation. In Revelation the viewpoint is different because it is the operation of the saints that is being considered; in Daniel we are thinking more from the standpoint of the nations and Israel.)

In Daniel Chapter 12, then, we have three unequal periods of about 3½ years each. We have already discovered that the first period (vs. 7) is the length of time Antichrist persecutes the saints. This is exactly the same length as that given in Revelation 12 and 13, for in both cases it is the saints that are involved. In both Daniel and Revelation this first period is 1260 days, or 3½ prophetic years.

Next is mentioned the last of the three periods of 3½ years, the one that begins with the abomination of desolation (vs. 11). This period starts in the middle of Daniel's 70th week and runs to the end of that "week." The exact number of days is 1290. During this period the two witnesses prophesy for 42 months (1260 days or 3½ years). Revelation 11:3 says, "I will give power unto my two witnesses, and they shall prophesy a thousand two hundred and three score days, clothed in sackcloth." Approximately 3½ years is also the length of time Jerusalem will be trodden under foot by the Gentiles. This period would have to be the last half of Daniel's 70th week. It is the second woe. (The third woe is the 7th trumpet.) So the 1260 days take us up to the blowing of the seventh trumpet. Some time would be required for the events under the 7th trumpet.

The thousand three hundred and five and thirty days. Between these two extremes is a second period, which, according to verse thirteen, lasts 1335 days. We are not told the exact events that mark the boundaries of this middle period of 3½ years, but it may start with the sealing of the 144,000, which takes place about 3½ years after the Rapture.

Some of the events covered by these three periods of time may be thought of as occurring somewhat instantaneously; others would take time. The Rapture, the resurrection of the tribulation saints, the return of Christ in glory, even the setting up the abomination of desolation, might be pinpointed to the day. But the sealing of the 144,000 takes some time, for the four angels hold in check the four winds of the earth saying, "Hurt not the earth, neither the sea, nor the trees, *till we have sealed the servants* of our God in their foreheads." If this sealing were instantaneous, there would be no need to hold back the wind till the sealing was completed. (The winds are the forerunners of the plagues.) The Battle of Armageddon will also take time, likewise, the setting up of the kingdom.

The only differences between the length of the times given here in Daniel and those given elsewhere are the time required to seal the 144,000 and the time required for the 7th trumpet.

THE END OF THE DAYS

But go thou thy way till the end be: for thou shalt rest, and stand in thy lot at the end of the days. —Dan. 12:13.

The *Septuagint* differs somewhat: "Go thy way and rest, for there are days and hours till the fulfillment of the end: and thou shalt rest and arise to thy glory at the end of the days."

And stand in thy lot. "Standing in the lot primarily suggests one's taking possession of what has been assigned by divine judgment." —*Pulpit Commentary*.

The end of the days. Daniel would rest in death but would stand in his lot—that is, he would rise from the dead in time to participate in the part assigned to him in the events of the last days.

INDEX TO SCRIPTURE REFERENCES

INDEX